The Nature of Leadership

Reptiles, Mammals, and the Challenge of
Becoming a Great Leader

B. Joseph White
President, University of Illinois

with Yaron Prywes

ᴧAMACOM

AMERICAN MANAGEMENT ASSOCIATION
New York • Atlanta • Brussels • Chicago • Mexico City • San Francisco
Shanghai • Tokyo • Toronto • Washington, D.C.

Special discounts on bulk quantities of AMACOM books are available to corporations, professional associations, and other organizations. For details, contact Special Sales Department, AMACOM, a division of American Management Association, 1601 Broadway, New York, NY 10019.
Tel.: 212-903-8316. Fax: 212-903-8083.
Website: www. amacombooks.org

This publication is designed to provide accurate and authoritative information in regard to the subject matter covered. It is sold with the understanding that the publisher is not engaged in rendering legal, accounting, or other professional service. If legal advice or other expert assistance is required, the services of a competent professional person should be sought.

Library of Congress Cataloging-in-Publication Data

White, B. Joseph.
    The nature of leadership : reptiles, mammals, and the challenge of becoming a great leader / B. Joseph White with Yaron Prywes.
        p.   cm.
    Includes bibliographical references and index.
    ISBN-13: 978-0-8144-0894-0
    ISBN-10: 0-8144-0894-X
    1. Leadership.   2. Success in business.   I. Prywes, Yaron.   II. Title.
    HD57.7.W458   2007
    658.4'092—dc22   2006015403

Printing number

10   9   8   7   6   5   4   3

***To my wife, Mary:**
Love of my life and the Great Leader of our family.*

CONTENTS

FOREWORD

Few social phenomena are as old, recognized as critical, and poorly understood as leadership. The importance of leadership is evident all through recorded human history. Leaders from Moses to Gandhi to Nelson Mandela transformed societies. While the study of leaders and leadership has a hoary tradition, an understanding of *how to become a leader* has remained an elusive question. To help people consciously build on their latent leadership potential, we have to go beyond traits and attributes such as personal values, style, courage, and passion. Joe White, in this book, has undertaken the tough task of articulating the *substance and measure* of leadership—the very soul of this complex phenomenon. And he has succeeded brilliantly.

Joe has more than 25 years experience as an academic and a leader of great academic institutions, as a manager in manufacturing and financial services, and as a board member with ample opportunities to exercise leadership and reflect on it. This combination of a *doer* and a *thinker* allows him a special vantage point from which to provide a new perspective. The core message of this book is profound and clear. The capacity to be focused on the *critical economic and performance issues* and at the same time be sensitive to the *social dimensions of leadership*—the reptilian "cold blooded" and the mammalian "warm and caring"—is at the core of leadership. Leaders learn to execute flawlessly and at the same time motivate through an exciting vision for the organization, to be efficient and also be innovative—thus *blending harmoniously* apparently contradictory capabilities. Ultimately, leadership is about change and transformation. Status quo is a sign of failure.

Joe has succeeded not just in providing a new and rich roadmap for personal development for those who want to lead but in cleverly weaving concepts, illustrations from his own experience, and a conversational style that makes these lessons easily accessible to all. His excitement and his experiences are motivating. By breaking the myth of birth, academic credentials, and privilege as prerequisites to leadership, he has *democratized* it. "Yes you can" is the message.

The Nature of Leadership has set a new standard for how to communicate complex ideas. I do hope millions of young people, especially, will benefit from making this book their blueprint for personal development as leaders.

C.K. Prahalad
Paul and Ruth McCracken Distinguished
University Professor of Corporate Strategy
Stephen M. Ross School of Business
The University of Michigan

Become a Leader, a Better Leader, a Great Leader

I write this book for you, current and future leaders everywhere. My message is that whatever your starting point, you can become a leader, a better leader, and maybe even a great leader.

But there are requirements and conditions. No major achievement comes without effort and at least a little bit of luck. You need to do your part, and that's what this book is about: helping you position and develop yourself to have a shot at being a great leader.

Leadership matters. We need people like you, our best and brightest, to aspire to great leadership. The world's future, as played out every day in tens of thou-

sands of workplaces and millions of individual decisions and personal interactions, depends on who leads.
The directions leaders set, the results they achieve, and
the values and tone with which they imbue their organizations have a profound effect on the quality of our
world and our individual lives.

In leading, as in performing music or acting, there
is no substitute for learning by doing. But a mental map
of the leadership terrain, and a few pointers from an
experienced expert about how to traverse the terrain
successfully, can help. This book will be that map for
you. I hope it will contribute significantly to your
growth, development, effectiveness, and success.

I can be your guide because I've taken the leadership journey. For me, it continues today in my position
as president of the University of Illinois. The university has campuses in Chicago, Urbana-Champaign, and
Springfield. It has 28,000 faculty and staff, 70,000 students, half a million alumni, and an annual budget of
nearly $4 billion. Since becoming university president
on January 31, 2005, I've reflected deeply on what I
have learned about leadership as I strive to make a
great institution even better in the years ahead. This
is a challenge because the University of Illinois has a
distinguished history academically (our faculty and
alumni have been awarded twenty-one Nobel Prizes),
culturally, and athletically.

Fortunately, I have a lot of experience on which to
draw. Over the last thirty years I have studied and practiced leadership as a professor, dean, corporate executive, and director or trustee of major public and private
companies and health care organizations. I have also
had the opportunity to be up close with some of world's

most famous leaders, including Steve Jobs, Archbishop Desmond Tutu, Herb Kelleher of Southwest Airlines, former Secretary of State Madeleine Albright, and many more. Now I want to share with you the leadership lessons I have learned.

I write this book not only for current and aspiring leaders. I also write it for those of you responsible for spotting, hiring, developing, evaluating, and occasionally firing leaders. You are the directors, trustees, and senior managers of companies and other organizations. You are human resources executives charged with management development. You are the voters in presidential, gubernatorial, and mayoral elections. You play a crucial role in deciding who in the world gets to be in charge, to whom we entrust our organizations and institutions, and upon whom we bestow the great privileges and serious responsibilities of leadership.

GREAT LEADERSHIP: NECESSARY AND SUFFICIENT CONDITIONS

For years, people have asked me, "What does it take to lead successfully?" My short answer has always been: "Just do three things. First, set high aspirations for your organization. Second, recruit great people. And third, bring tremendous energy and enthusiasm to work every day."

It's a good answer, but it's incomplete. This book is intended to be a much better answer to the question.

Leadership is a high calling and it can be very fulfilling. Leadership, as I have experienced it, is also fast-paced and fun, and I want this book to be the same. That's why I decided to organize it around something that puts a smile on my face: animals.

I'll introduce you to the Reptile side of leadership and to the Mammal side. The Reptile and Mammal metaphors can help us visualize the enormous variety of challenges that leaders face, and how to deal with them effectively.

Leadership involves the head and the heart. It is both analytical and interpersonal. Having the range and repertoire to be cold-blooded, rational, and decisive at times, and at other times warm-blooded, nurturing, and participative, and knowing when to be which, is a huge personal challenge. It's right up there with running marathons or learning to play the violin well. Or more accurately, running marathons *and* playing the violin well.

To be a *good* leader, you have to be as tough as nails (this is what I call Reptilian excellence) and warm as toast (what I call Mammalian excellence). Achieving both kinds of excellence is a necessary but not sufficient condition of being a *great* leader.

So what is the sufficient condition? Let's put the answer right up front. To be a great leader, you have to be successful at *achieving change*—important, consequential change in the results for which you are responsible. Making change successfully is a leader's greatest challenge.

It is not by accident that America's greatest presidents—Washington, Lincoln, and Roosevelt—all led winning wars that produced great and positive change: the birth of a nation, the elimination of slavery, the defeat of tyranny. To be a great leader your results have to be excellent—you have to win—and your results need to produce consequential change.

Thus, we remember Jack Welch, former chairman of General Electric (and a University of Illinois graduate), as a great value creator. We think of Steve Jobs as a tremendous innovator of products we care about, like Macintosh computers and iPods and Pixar animated films. We admire a person like Wendy Kopp, the founder of Teach for America, because she married up the idealistic ambitions of thousands of young college graduates with the desperate need for better education among America's underprivileged children. We look up to Archbishop Desmond Tutu for his leading role, with Nelson Mandela, in achieving a bloodless end to apartheid in South Africa, a magnificent moral and political achievement.

There are also thousands of great leaders we've never heard of. They are the people—heroes in my book—who turn around an underperforming school or classroom or lead a work group in any organization to new heights of performance and pride.

To illustrate, let me tell you about a great leader you may never have heard of who heads an organization of which you probably *have* heard. His name is Mannie Jackson, and he heads the Harlem Globetrotters.

THE MANNIE JACKSON STORY

I know Mannie Jackson's story because Mannie is a graduate of the University of Illinois. He is one of the most inspiring people I've ever met. He told me his story recently in a long lunch in Phoenix that I'll never forget.

Mannie grew up in the forties and fifties, an African-American in a small town in southern Illinois. His father was an autoworker. Mannie was a good student and a star high school basketball player. On the strength of these qualifications, he came to the University of Illinois in Urbana-Champaign in the mid-1950s to go to school and play basketball as one of the university's first African-American players. He did well as a student and as an athlete, serving his senior year as co-captain of the Fighting Illini basketball team.

At our lunch, Mannie told me that the University of Illinois was his gateway to the world and a life of high achievement.

After graduation, Mannie Jackson played basketball for a year and a half for the Harlem Globetrotters and its famous owner, Abe Saperstein. Mannie told me that Abe took him under his wing and since, in Mannie's opinion, Saperstein was the greatest promoter who ever lived, Mannie learned a lot about the Globetrotters' business.

Mannie went on to a great thirty-year career at Honeywell, Inc. in Minneapolis. As a senior executive of a major company, he learned about marketing, operations, finance, and general management. Then, in the early 1990s, at just the age when a lot of his peers were retiring to Florida to play golf, Mannie Jackson did something different. He left Honeywell and bought the Harlem Globetrotters, the team for which he had once played. (Is this an only-in-America story or what?)

Eight years later, Mannie wrote about his experience buying, owning, and turning around the Globetrotters in a *Harvard Business Review* article entitled "Bringing a Dying Brand Back to Life," which is what the Harlem Globetrotters business was when Mannie acquired it. He took a big risk, envisioned how the team could once again be successful, then went about the hard work of making it so. He put together a strategy and plan, recruited the right people to work with him, then worked hard for a decade to execute the plan and turn the organization around. He succeeded . . . big time.

What Mannie Jackson did is what all great leaders do. They spot a need or opportunity or simply develop a passion. They take a risk. They envision what positive, consequential change will look like and what will be needed to achieve it. They put together a plan. They recruit great people to work with them. Then they work hard, hope and pray for a little wind at their backs, celebrate successes when they happen, and overcome adversity when it occurs—as it always does. They measure their success in the change they make and the results they achieve—strong results over a sustained period.

That's great leadership.

HOW TO USE THIS BOOK TO BECOME A GREAT LEADER

Now you know what it means to *be* a great leader. But you don't yet know the secret of *becoming* a great leader. That's the purpose of this book: to position and prepare you to have a shot at becoming a great leader.

How do you go from your starting point—whatever it is—to being a winner in the leadership sweepstakes? And how do you use this book to achieve that goal?

There are three important steps:

- Remember that there is a difference between leadership and management.

- Ask and answer these questions: Can I really develop myself to be a great leader? And will I have the chance to serve as one?

- Challenge yourself to climb the Leadership Pyramid.

Remember there is a difference between leadership and management. Leading is not the same as managing, and being a good manager doesn't necessarily guarantee leadership success. Management is fundamentally about *order and control.* Leadership is fundamentally about *achieving goals and making change.*

I once served on a board of directors in which we were discussing a member of senior management who was performing well but left us wanting more. He was competent, well-organized, attentive, hardworking, earnest, and in control. So what's to want, you might ask? Another director put it perfectly: "He's a good manager, but can he become a leader?"

Management requires planning, organizing, directing, and controlling. These functions are vital to an organization's well-being since they provide a script, roles, guidance, and feedback to the organizational actors. But these managerial functions by themselves will not ensure superb organizational performance any more than a script, roles, guidance, and feedback will make the difference between a competent high-school-quality rendition of *West Side Story* and a great Broadway revival of the show.

Leadership, on the other hand, requires native talent, developed abilities, and the ephemeral but critical qualities of vision, inspiration, imagination, innovation, risk-taking, perspective, passion, excitement, and chemistry. Although both leadership and management abilities can be developed, I believe the odds are much better to develop acceptable managerial abilities in budding leaders (or, alternatively, to surround exciting leaders with able managers) than to try and develop deep leadership capability in competent managers.

Nonetheless, given the intertwined nature of leadership and management, and the fact that both types of abilities can be developed to some degree, it is important to carefully assess whether an individual's shortcomings are more in the managerial or leadership realms and what development efforts are likely to shore them up.

Ask yourself, Can I really develop myself to be a great leader? And will I have the chance to serve as one? Let me give you the answers. Odds are they are "Yes, if you really want to," and "Yes."

Let's take the second question first; it's simpler. The world is chronically short of people with extraordinary leadership ability. I know because I've been on the demand side of the equation so often and for so long. From where I sit, demand for excellent leaders is high. While young people understandably worry "Can I get a job?" more senior people such as executives, board members, and search committee members wonder, "Why aren't there more wonderful candidates from which to choose the next CEO (or department chair or head coach)? Why do we have to compromise more than we want to?"

I'll bet you've had this experience yourself. Have you ever looked at the candidates for the world's most powerful job, president of the United States, and thought, "Can't we do better?"

I've learned over the years that there are a lot of smart people. And there are a lot of well-educated people and people with good-looking resumes. But there is a serious shortage of people who are highly effective at the practice of leadership, people who can achieve positive, consequential change by inspiring us and mobilizing us; high-integrity people who make commitments carefully and keep them faithfully; people who are both tough and smart, yet warm and caring. These are the kinds of people to whom we want to entrust our organizations, ourselves, our children, and our futures. There are not enough of them, and this shortage is your opportunity!

As for whether you can develop yourself to be a great leader, I said the answer is "Yes, if you *really* want to." Here are a few thoughts for you to consider as you make that decision.

There is a critically important, fork-in-the-road career decision you will face a few times in your life that will rule you in or out of the leadership sweepstakes. The decision is whether to be primarily an *individual contributor* in your work or primarily a *leader of others*. To become a great leader, the first requirement is to opt, at some time, for leadership work rather than, or in addition to, individual contributor work.

Some people can't wait for this opportunity; they're dying to be in charge. Others wouldn't dream of it; they love their craft and don't want the distractions and hassles of supervision, management, and leadership. (This is the reason that in colleges and universities, newly appointed deans and department heads receive messages of condolence as well as congratulations from their faculty colleagues who have happily opted for the individual contributor path.) But you can't run the leadership race unless you get on the leadership track. And although it is true that people can exercise leadership in any role or from any perch, my focus in this book is on people in *formal* positions of leadership: supervisors, managers, and executives.

After you've contemplated the option of being a leader and decided to give it a go, you'll find that there are some things for which you have natural talents. Maybe your strengths are setting goals and direction, or recruiting and motivating people, or analyzing and solving problems, or being tough and decisive in difficult situations. You'll become known for the things you're good at and you'll do them a lot. That's good.

But it's also bad. Because there will inevitably be things that fully developed leaders need to do that don't come naturally to you. If, and only if, you learn what those are and learn, as they say in sports, to "play to your weak side," will you have a shot at being a complete leader. And being complete is a precondition to greatness.

Leaders: Born or Made?

An interesting, ongoing research project looking at identical twins reared apart suggests there is a genetic component to leadership potential.[1] Nevertheless, it's still up to you to make the most of your talents for leadership.

Challenge yourself to climb the Leadership Pyramid. In Chapter 3, I present the Leadership Pyramid as a simple way to organize your journey to become a great leader. At the base of the pyramid are the foundation requirements. You don't qualify to become a great leader unless you really want to be in charge and have the requisite ability, strength, and character.

At the next level of the pyramid, you need to master the Reptilian and Mammalian requirements of leadership. At the top of the pyramid is the challenge of making change: being innovative, taking risks, recruiting great people, maintaining perspective, and developing that personal "something extra" that sets great leaders apart from the rest of us.

Leaders are high-achieving people. They love challenges and have rarely seen a hill of any kind that they don't want to climb. It's not coincidence that most leaders love competition of all kinds (why else do successful business people buy professional sports teams?) and are attracted to various kinds of self-improvement, from pursuing athletic endeavors to collecting art to learning to play the piano.

For such people (and I expect you're one), the Leadership Pyramid is a wonderful developmental challenge. You can climb all the way to the top but you'll never completely master it. There is always more to learn. Just when you think you know everything you can about some element of the pyramid—being on top of the numbers or communicating well or developing a "helicopter view"—you'll get some feedback or have an experience that reminds you that you're not quite as good as you thought. You can never, ever get it all right. And of course, throughout your professional life you will face the challenge of applying your leadership abilities to new and changing situations.

HOW TO USE YOUR LIFE TO BECOME A GREAT LEADER

The Leadership Pyramid identifies a full range of talents and abilities you'll need to develop to have a shot at being a great leader. But it won't be enough just to read about them any more than reading about playing the violin or running a marathon will get you ready for a recital or a race. You are going to have to try things out, listen to and observe others, and practice, practice, practice. This is what professional development is all about: going from conceptual understanding to behavioral mastery. How to do it? There's no simple answer, but here are some good ideas.

First, be open to and seek out dead-honest feedback from those who know you best. A few months after I took my first leadership job as an officer at Cummins Engine Company, a fellow came into my office, closed the door, and said, "I've been watching you in meetings. I think you're really uncomfortable with conflict. You're always trying to smooth things over or patch them up, usually prematurely. Get used to conflict and learn how engage it. If you don't, you might as well hang it up." Good insight! Fine advice! I worked at it, and for years now I've been able to sit without flinching in the heaviest conflict situations. In fact, when I think it's worth doing, I even stir up the conflict myself.

Second, find a great organization in which to work and a great person for whom to work. We learn about leading by observing and practicing. Learning from the best all day, every day, is by far the most powerful teacher. I have admired and tried to incorporate into my own approach many qualities I saw in my former bosses, colleagues, and other associates. I've marveled at Madeleine Albright's pioneering achievements, Steve Jobs's creativity and aesthetic sense, Herb Kelleher's laugh and love of people, and Desmond Tutu's charisma and saintliness. Observing these people and their admirable qualities has been instrumental to my own growth as a leader.

By the way, although it is vital to learn from good bosses in good organizations, odds are that like me, you'll also spend a little time in lousy organizations and have a few insufferable bosses. That's okay; you can learn a lot about who you want to be by being crystal clear about who you *don't* want to be! I hit a low point with one boss when he told me the only way to motivate people is through fear and intimidation, then proceeded to berate me for having lunch with my wife on a workday! (I found I was only motivated to resign.)

You can also learn a lot from visible leadership failures. For example, has any American president ever squandered more natural talent and opportunity than Bill Clinton, who was undone by his lack of integrity and self-discipline? Did leaders learn from George H. W. Bush's loss to Bill Clinton that they shouldn't make important promises ("no new taxes") then not keep them?

Let's not forget that in the business world, 30 percent to 50 percent of CEOs are prematurely ousted.[2] Interestingly, researchers have found that the key difference between successful and derailed executives is their ability to learn from experience, including mistakes and failures.[3]

Finally, you need to learn as much as possible about what I call the leadership game. You need to encounter a variety of situations: having a big lead, being way behind, encountering various kinds of teammates and opponents, playing in different kinds of weather (Is your workplace stormy or sunny?), figuring out how to have both a good game plan and superb execution. Knowing what situation you are in as a leader, and having well-developed insights and instincts about the right way to deal with it, can contribute enormously to your effectiveness.

Did You Know?

Nearly three-quarters of employees (65 percent to 75 percent) report that the worst and most stressful aspect of their job is their immediate boss. Complaints include the boss's inability to make decisions and face conflict, and tendency to tyrannize subordinates (i.e., "Manager supervises too closely," "Treats me like I'm stupid").[4]

J. Irwin Miller, who built Cummins Engine Company from a small company in Columbus, Indiana, into the world's largest independent manufacturer of diesel engines, used to say to those of us in senior management, "If the folks on the shop floor don't understand what you're saying, then *you* don't know what you're talking about!" Irwin was a master of the short, declarative sentence, plain language, and vivid examples. His clarity in communicating is my standard in writing this book.

Let's get started.

CHAPTER

The Reptiles versus
the Mammals

Dichotomies are deeply embedded in human thought and traditions of all kinds. We love to think and talk in terms of black and white. Women are from Venus, men are from Mars. Liberals versus conservatives. Main Street and Wall Street. Good versus evil. Hard and soft. Us and them. Yin and yang. Want more? Try internal versus external, stability versus change, freedom and control.

Consider politics: Is government the problem or the solution? Does preemptive war increase our security or decrease it? Consider religion: the inclusive, ecumenical, change-embracing branches of Christianity,

Judaism, and Islam versus the exclusive, isolationist, preservationist branches of each faith. Even in the institutional mainstream, there are dualities and efforts to reconcile them. Consider the centrist striving of the Democratic Leadership Council under Bill Clinton ("fiscally conservative, socially progressive") and the "compassionate conservatism" of George W. Bush.

DICHOTOMIES AND THE WORLD OF WORK

I first encountered dichotomies in the world of leadership and management when I was a student at the Harvard Business School: Theory X and Theory Y. This was Douglas McGregor's formulation in the 1950s in a book called *The Human Side of Enterprise.* In a nutshell, McGregor said that if managers believe that people are fundamentally lazy, dishonest, and not trustworthy, they will motivate and manage through fear, intimidation, and control (Theory X). If, by contrast, managers believe that people are fundamentally hardworking, honorable, and trustworthy, then they will motivate and manage through respect, involvement, and delegation (Theory Y).

This notion of how managers' own philosophies influence the way they treat people intrigued me. I immediately wondered, of course, about complications, like some people being saints and others being scoundrels and the same person sometimes being a saint and other times a scoundrel. But these nuances could wait.

My next exposure to dichotomies in management

came in the work of Frederick Herzberg, a Case Western University professor who created the Hygiene/ Motivator Theory. Herzberg's claim, based on some research he had done in various workplaces, was that there is one set of things important to people at work, such as security, pay, and working conditions (Herzberg called them "hygiene" factors). If they aren't right, people will be *dissatisfied*. But even if management could get all these things right, people would only be *not dissatisfied*. They wouldn't be highly *satisfied* and, importantly, they wouldn't be motivated to do a great job. Satisfaction and motivation, according to Herzberg, require quite a different set of things that he called "motivators"—in particular, good leadership, challenging work, and recognition.

Herzberg's work was widely discredited in the years after he published it by researchers who tried to nail down and replicate his findings. But managers loved it—it made intuitive sense to them—and I have found it to be useful and generally valid in my leadership experience. I would say, in fact, that you can attract many people with good pay and working conditions, and they can be attracted away if you don't have these things. But getting the best out of people requires more. It requires leadership they admire, work that stretches and develops them, and appreciation and recognition (especially by the leader) of their achievements.

One of the most widely known leadership dichotomy frameworks is Blake and Mouton's Leadership Grid,[1] which is shown in Figure 2-1.

Why are we so attracted to dichotomies? Mainly, I

Figure 2-1. A popular leadership dichotomy: people vs. production.

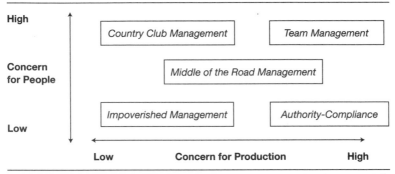

SOURCE: Robert R. Blake and Anne A. McCanse, *Leadership Dilemmas-Grid Solutions* (Houston: Gulf Pub. Co., 1991).

think, because they help us simplify a messy and complicated world and make it more understandable and "discussable." For example, Melanie Klein, a psychoanalyst in the 1920s, introduced the concept of "splitting," the psychological mechanism of dividing complex feelings into differentiated elements. She argued that by splitting emotions, children gain relief from internal conflicts such as deep ambivalence toward parents. I actually saw splitting first hand years ago when my then five-year-old son, Brian, told my wife and me about his two imaginary friends, Ernin, a very good boy, and Sam, a nasty, naughty boy. Talk about dichotomy! For about a year, Brian attributed his good behavior to Ernin's influence and blamed Sam for his naughtiness. (If this report about Brian's psyche leaves you concerned, I'm pleased to report that he is now thirty-two with a well-integrated personality and his own children, whose psyches he is busy sorting out.)

Dichotomies are, by their nature, simple and simplistic, useful and misleading, at best partially valid and always incomplete. We should remember that they can have serious consequences. For example, in the hands of unscrupulous, demagogic leaders, dichotomous language—"us versus them"—can open the door to discrimination, abuse, torture, and even genocide. But dichotomies, used constructively, can interest, instruct, and entertain us. They can stimulate new ways for us to think and speak about familiar things. They can be very useful in helping us coin convenient, memorable language . . . language like "Reptile leaders" and "Mammal leaders." Let me explain.

THE SOFTBALL TEAMS

In the 1990s, I was dean of the University of Michigan Business School. Being dean of a top business school is an interesting job. You're surrounded by faculty, students, and staff who are smart and independent. Because your job is to get them moving in roughly the same direction, some people describe being dean as the professional equivalent of "herding cats." But I never found it that way.

Rather, I figured my job was to understand what made everybody tick, then appeal both to their highest collective aspirations ("We intend to be the world's best business school and be recognized as such") and to their most selfish ("No one wants you to have an endowed chair, more colleagues, and a big research budget more than I do, but you'll have to do a great job of teaching, writing, and service if it's going to happen"). My job description, as I saw it, was simple: I would help the members of the school community make their individual dreams come true in exchange for their helping make our collective dreams for the school come true.

Given this way of thinking, I always had my ear to the ground for insights that would enable me to understand the community and the people I was charged to lead. Early in my tenure as dean, I got a big one.

Each summer, after the students had graduated or gone off to their internships, we had a picnic for faculty and staff and their families. I loved those picnics. You'd see your professional colleagues in a different guise: wearing jeans and shorts, with kids and dogs in tow, warm and relaxed on a lazy summer day in a bucolic setting.

On the day of the school picnic, workplace differences were set aside. Or so I thought.

One summer, shortly before the picnic, I saw an e-mail announcing a faculty softball game. It was going to be "the Reptiles versus the Mammals." This intrigued me. On closer reading, I noticed that the captain of the Reptiles was also the chair of the accounting department. The captain of the Mammals was the chair of the organizational behavior (read "human relations") department.

It turned out that the two captains, Gene and Jim, had organized the game and named the teams. As I suspected, there was nothing accidental about the choice of names. Words, after all, are the raw material of faculty work! The Reptiles were composed mainly of faculty trained in economics and were thus drawn from disciplines such as accounting, finance, and business economics. The Mammals were mainly faculty trained in the behavioral sciences and drawn from departments with a human relations orientation, such as organizational behavior and marketing.

As with all dichotomies, this one was not perfect. Where do you put the business law and operations management faculty? (Probably with the Reptiles.) Where do you put the communications faculty and the business ethicists? (Probably with the Mammals.) But these are details.

As dean, I thought the idea of the Reptiles versus the Mammals in softball was hilarious and extremely clever. Anyone who knew anything about business and business schools immediately got it. It was the analytical, numbers-oriented, flinty-eyed (not to say cold and calculating) faculty versus the holistic, people-oriented, dewy-eyed (not to say naïve and bad-at-math) faculty. And of course, the visual imagery evoked by these names is terrific. Here's what came to my mind:

Reptile *versus* Mammal

I'm sure you want to know who won the softball game. It turns out there were actually two games. The

Reptiles won the first game, 8–3. The Mammals won the second, 12–10. Sorry, no universal conclusions to be drawn yet about the dominance of Reptiles versus Mammals, at least in softball.

By the way, I discovered in piecing together the history of the Reptiles and Mammals the advantage of having a Reptile as captain of a softball team. Gene, the accounting professor, immediately remembered the precise scores of these inconsequential games that occurred a decade ago. I also got a glimpse into the mind of a Mammal. Jim had no idea what the score was (or even that there were two games), but he did remember a human matter. He reminded me that he had successfully recruited our senior associate dean, Ted Snyder, who was a great athlete and a University of Chicago Ph.D. economist (and later became dean of Chicago's Graduate School of Business), and thus a gold-plated Reptile, to join the Mammals.

The Reptiles and Mammals faculty softball teams stimulated lines of thought in my mind that continue to develop today. They didn't quite represent a moment of blinding insight, like the biblical story of Saul being struck down by God on the road to Damascus, but for me it was close to that.

BUSINESS SCHOOL CULTURE: ENGINEERS AND POETS

Faculty at top business schools share the same curriculum, facilities, parking lot, and a focus on business. But their different intellectual orientations, rooted in their doctoral training, result in views about companies, people, and the business world that could hardly be more different.

Faculty trained in economics focus heavily on the market, the rules of the competitive game, cost/benefit analysis, incentives, enforceable contracts, and unintended consequences. They see firms as profit-maximizing economic entities and people as rational economic actors. By contrast, faculty members trained in other social sciences tend to see companies as human communities. They focus on the individual and the group, emotions, complex motivation, communication, influence and persuasion, and networks.

There are quiet tensions between these two points of view and their proponents. Economics-oriented faculty, a.k.a. the Reptiles, tend to think of their non-economist colleagues as lightweights, soft, weak on analysis, and somewhat naïve. The Mammals on the faculty tend to think of their Reptile colleagues as theoretical, humorless, and out of touch with the richness of real people and organizations.

Parallel fault lines run in the student body: "the engineers and the poets," as the faculty like to call them. MBA classes involve a lot of discussion that lets you get to know your student colleagues and their views pretty well.

Let's say, for example, you have a case study that frames the question of whether management (you) ought to retain work in a small Midwestern community or outsource it to India. The "engineers" (i.e., undergraduate majors in engineering, science, and math) will quickly run the numbers and generally conclude that this decision is a no-brainer: The work goes to Bangalore, the sooner the better. Meanwhile, the undergraduate "poets" are deeply troubled by this decision and invoke every reason imaginable why the day of reckoning should be put off, hopefully forever.

It's Reptiles versus Mammals: cold, calculating, and rational versus warm, caring, and nurturing.

REPTILES AND MAMMALS: THE HUMAN METAPHOR

In the same way that we can learn deeply important things about work, family, and life from *Death of a Salesman* or about leadership, family, and tragedy from *King Lear,* we can learn a lot about critical dimensions of leadership from a Reptile versus Mammal metaphor. But before we get started, let me quickly state the obvious: My metaphor is not rooted in the science of reptiles and mammals. It is more literary than scientific.

In nature, real reptiles are cold-blooded creatures. They are ectothermic, which means their body temperatures are dependent on the temperature of their surroundings. They have an external covering of scales or horny plates. They usually lay eggs to reproduce. Mammals, which most scientists believe evolved from reptiles some 200 million years ago, are warm-blooded creatures. They are homeothermic, maintaining a relatively constant and warm body temperature independent of the temperature of their surroundings. Mammals have a covering of hair on the skin. Females bear live young and have milk-producing mammary glands for nourishing them.

And the workplace human counterparts of reptiles and mammals? In their pure types, I suggest that reptilian humans are primarily *detached, analytical, and critical* in their orientation toward issues and people at work. By contrast, mammalian humans are *engaged, emotional, and nurturing.* Reptiles tend to be *competitive and strive to dominate.* Mammals tend to be *cooperative and strive for consensus.* Reptiles are oriented toward *contracts and formality* when it comes to agreements among parties, while Mammals prefer *informal agreements and understandings* based on shared values and community needs.

Some of these differences are, to a degree, rooted in the intellectual differences between economists and financial types, on the one hand, and behavioral scientists and general management types on the other. Here are some examples:

Habits of the Mind

Reptiles	Mammals
Detached	Engaged
Analytical	Emotional
Quantitative	Qualitative
Independent	Interdependent
Adversarial	Cooperative

Focus on Control	Emphasis on Freedom
Faith in Evidence	Faith in Others
Rely on Audits	Rely on Trust
Value Contracts	Value Community

Human beings have long made connections between real and metaphorical reptiles and mammals. Truman Capote wrote a book about two heartless killers called *In Cold Blood*. We say that a person impervious to criticism is "thick-skinned" (think reptilian scales and plates) and that one overly sensitive is "thin-skinned" (think pink and naked mammal baby). We praise a citizen for "nurturing" young people in his charge or "giving back" to her community. We condemn people as snakes.

Attributing reptilian and mammalian characteristics to humans is deeply embedded in our thinking and language. It is not surprising, then, that when it comes to leadership, we are sensitive to the reptilian and mammalian dimensions of those to whom we look for guidance, direction, and protection, and as symbols of our values and aspirations.

REPTILES AND MAMMALS AT WORK

I got my first real job when I was sixteen, in a wholesale plumbing and construction warehouse in Kalamazoo,

Michigan. It was at Bond Supply Company that I first began thinking about the different orientations people bring to work.

A CEO Snake Charmer

In a 2003 article in *Fortune* magazine about Hank Paulson, then CEO of Goldman Sachs, the writer makes a big point about Paulson's deep interest in snakes. The article intertwines Paulson's love of these reptiles with his personal style and leadership of the firm.

> "I love . . ." he says sadly [after failing to find a snake that his guide has pointed out], his voice trailing off. "Snakes?" I ask. "Yes," he replies matter-of-factly. "I like to hold them and look at them."
>
> Wendy, his wife of thirty-four years, can immediately tell that Paulson has had a reptile experience. "He had that snake look in his eyes," she says.
>
> This is . . . one of the investment community's *steeliest, stealthiest* power brokers . . . he is also shaking up Goldman, working hard to make it *leaner and more aggressive* globally. [Emphasis added.][2]

I remember a retiree named Bert who came through the shop each morning, meticulously writing down our coffee and doughnut orders and collecting money to pay for them. An hour later, he would return and deliver the goods and our change, then sit with us and chat while we took a break. Bert had retired at least a decade earlier. But he'd come up with a great excuse to keep coming to work every day. Why? Obviously, work meant something more than pay to him. (Score one for the Mammals!) It meant people, service, maybe even a vital connection with reality. Bert was a workplace Mammal. The company was his community and he helped maintain it with outreach, warmth, and caring.

There are also workplace Reptiles. They come to work to do a good job and get paid. Everything else is secondary. I saw a great illustration of this one evening at my wife's and my favorite neighborhood bar, Brandy's, on East 84th Street in New York City. At Brandy's there's an excellent piano player, the bartenders and wait staff do the singing, and they're all amazing performers. Tips are an important part of their compensation. One of the server/singers is a woman with great warmth and a terrific voice. Her performance the night we were there was spectacular and the crowd was really into it. We were cheering and calling for an encore. She accepted our adulation graciously and then said, "Thanks. I appreciate your love. But I come to work to earn money. I have a great husband and I get plenty of affection at home. I'd appreciate your generosity." Score one for the Reptiles! Despite her warm demeanor, this wonderful performer is first and foremost a workplace Reptile, doing her job more for money than for love.

NOT BETTER, NOT WORSE, JUST DIFFERENT

I hope it's clear through these two illustrations that I make no judgment about the inherent value of Reptiles and Mammals in the workplace. Both are vital and most people are, of course, a complex mix of the two. We need task-oriented, no-nonsense Reptiles to ensure the work gets done and done well. We need people-oriented, nurturing Mammals to maintain the human community through which work gets done. We need both and there's room for both, as long as the Reptiles meet a threshold of civility and the Mammals produce good work. There are, of course, problem Reptiles (selfish and destructive) and problem Mammals (slackers and gossips). And that raises an important distinction I want to draw here.

I have noticed that many people with whom I've spoken about the Reptile and Mammal metaphor attribute "good" to Mammals and "bad" to Reptiles. This instinctive reaction may be rooted in our common aversion to snakes and lizards and our attraction to puppies and kittens. The bias is reinforced in literature and countless works of art, mainly religious, that portray reptiles as evil (e.g., the devil appears as a serpent). But workplace Reptiles and Mammals, including Reptile and Mammal *leaders,* are no more inherently good or bad than their animal counterparts. This point will become important when we discuss leaders, because I believe organizations falter, fail, or don't reach their potential *both* because of leadership that is inadequately Reptilian *and* because of leadership that is inadequately Mammalian. So from the outset, let's dispel the notion that Mammal = good and Reptile = bad. Oh, if only it were that simple!

BOTH CRITICAL

The best leaders must be both Reptilian and Mammalian. Here's why:

Leaders must be *Reptilian* because organizations are challenged to survive in a competitive, Darwinian environment and because they are populated by fallible human beings who are, at times, negligent, fraudulent, ornery, and bullying.

Leaders must be *Mammalian* because organizations are composed of human beings who are free to choose the organizations with which they affiliate (it helps leaders to think of employees as volunteers), possess the knowledge and ideas the organization needs to thrive, are capable of amazing and wonderful things, and are hungry for inspiration, challenge, achievement, and recognition.

Leaders must be *Reptilian* because people need order, stability, routines, and resources in order to perform productively, reliably, and efficiently.

Leaders must be *Mammalian* because people need attention, room to grow, and someone to believe in them in order to do their best, learn, and be creative.

Leaders must be *Reptilian* in order to establish authority and exercise power. They must be *Mammalian* because people deserve to be treated with dignity and respect.

Leaders must be *Reptilian* to stand up to a harsh and threatening competitive environment. They must be *Mammalian* to embrace and empathize with suffering humanity.

Leaders must be *Reptilian* because organizations

need good management. They must be *Mammalian* because people deserve good leadership.

Reptilian leadership improves the odds that an organization will survive. *Mammalian* leadership improves the odds that an organization will thrive.

Reptiles and Mammals represent two sides of the Leadership Pyramid, which is straight ahead.

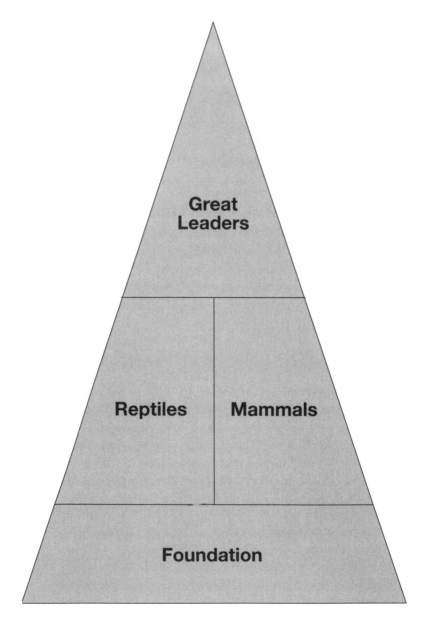

CHAPTER 3

The Leadership Pyramid

Over the years, I have seen many approaches that companies and other organizations use to select, evaluate, train, and cultivate their managers—in other words, to develop leaders. These approaches range in quality from good to awful. One thing that nearly all share is that they are far too complex.

I introduce here a simple but comprehensive model of leadership development. I call it the Leadership Pyramid. The pyramid helps you identify your natural strengths and your weaknesses (we all have them!). It can help you develop your strengths, improve on your weaknesses, and guide you to leadership excellence.

The pyramid (as shown in Figure 3-1) has four components:

- *Foundation Requirements.* To be a leader, you must have a great desire to be in charge. This is not necessarily ego-driven. Usually it springs from a personal belief that you could guide, organize, and support others effectively to accomplish a goal—win a ball game, raise money, build a company, win an election. Three other qualities determine your probabilities of success as a leader: ability, strength, and character.

- *Reptilian Requirements.* This is the vital *hard* side of leadership work. Its foundation is good economic sense combined with financial management skills, an instinct to verify (audit) what is being reported as reality, and a strong penchant for control, follow-up, and attention to detail. This approach requires rational analysis, discipline, and toughness.

- *Mammalian Requirements.* This is the vital *soft* side of leadership work. It requires "people sense" that rests on good intuition and genuine empathy, the ability to put oneself in another's shoes. Its foundation is communication skills, both listening and "broadcasting" in writing, speaking, and nonverbal terms. This approach is characterized by warm engagement and nurturing others to learn, grow, develop, and succeed.

- *Great Leader Requirements.* This is *the* work of leadership at the highest level. It is about making consequential and successful change. The top of the pyramid assumes that you have the ability to be hard and soft and the instincts and experience to know what

Figure 3-1. The Leadership Pyramid.

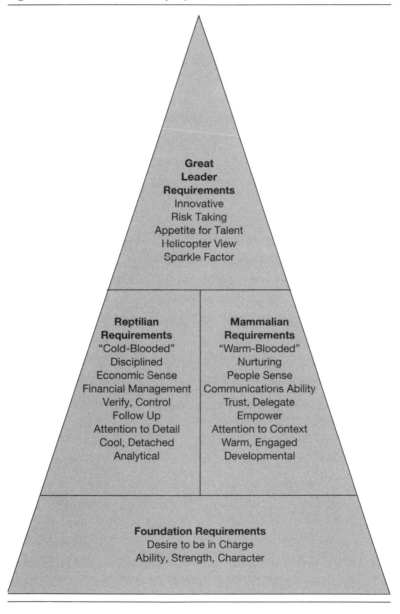

Great
Leader
Requirements
Innovative
Risk Taking
Appetite for Talent
Helicopter View
Sparkle Factor

Reptilian
Requirements
"Cold-Blooded"
Disciplined
Economic Sense
Financial Management
Verify, Control
Follow Up
Attention to Detail
Cool, Detached
Analytical

Mammalian
Requirements
"Warm-Blooded"
Nurturing
People Sense
Communications Ability
Trust, Delegate
Empower
Attention to Context
Warm, Engaged
Developmental

Foundation Requirements
Desire to be in Charge
Ability, Strength, Character

each situation requires. Because great leaders are change makers, they are also innovators and intelligent risk takers. They have a boundless appetite to recruit and work with the most talented people. They possess a rare sense of perspective or "helicopter view." And they have a personal something special—presence, energy, charisma—that I call the "sparkle factor."

PEOPLE OF THE PYRAMID

When I look at the Leadership Pyramid, I see people.

Archbishop Desmond Tutu of South Africa is the most remarkable Mammal leader I ever met. I spent time with him in Cape Town during a break in the hearings of the Truth and Reconciliation Commission that he was chairing. When I arrived, he was leading the singing of "Happy Birthday" to a staff member. His people clearly adored him. He radiated warmth and joy. This was remarkable to me because he had spent the morning listening to wrenching stories from apartheid victims and their families of the deepest hatred and most heartless brutality that human beings can impose on each other.

We spoke for forty-five minutes. I will never forget the Archbishop telling me the role that God, prayer, the churches, and good people of all faiths played in bringing an end to apartheid. Nor, since my mission was to discuss business development and economic opportunity in South Africa, will I forget his telling me that success on this front was vital, because without the progress represented by, for example, a new water pipe in a township or the possibility of a job, South Africa could slide into chaos.

Many of the best Reptilian leaders become chief financial officers. One great CFO who stands out in my mind is David Neithercut, now the chief executive officer of Equity Residential (NYSE: EQR), America's largest apartment real estate investment trust. I met Dave when I became an EQR trustee at the time it went public in 1993. Dave and I became well acquainted because I chaired the EQR audit committee and he was CFO. Dave was only thirty-seven years old when we met, and I was bowled over by his financial acumen and the quickness of his mind. He had just the right pedigree for a Reptilian leader: a Columbia University MBA in accounting and finance. Dave dazzled the board with his recitations on EQR's capital structure and complex financing arrangements. But more important, we knew that with Dave in charge of the balance sheet, not a single detail would go unnoticed or be left to chance. Indeed, it used to give me comfort as a trustee that this young man who could wow them on Wall Street had an unconscious habit of carrying a sharpened, yellow no. 2 pencil over his ear just like a green-eyeshade-wearing bookkeeper!

Henry Schacht, the CEO of Cummins Engine when I joined the company, was my personal introduction to a Great Leader. Straight-backed, square-jawed, brilliant, ethical, articulate, and persuasive, Henry had it all in a way I had never before encountered. As a Great Leader, Henry forged a compelling competitive strategy requiring massive change for Cummins, he was always on top of the numbers, and he communicated superbly to all the company's constituents. These were givens. More striking to me was how tough and steady Henry was on the one hand and, on the other, how intensely he focused on and extended attention and respect to every individual he encountered. I had never seen anything quite like it.

Let me explain.

I discovered when I went from academic life into senior management work what an emotional roller coaster the latter is. The ups-and-downs don't come over a period of weeks or months, as they tend to in our personal lives, forming what we think of as "the good times" and "the bad times." In leadership, the ups-and-downs come the way a prizefighter must experience them in the ring: absorbing blows and dishing out punishment nearly simultaneously, multiple times in a three-minute round. This reminds me of an ancient Jewish folktale: King Solomon commissioned a jeweler to make a ring with an inscription, the words of which would be meaningful whatever the situation, good or bad. The jeweler brought him a ring with the words: "This too shall pass."

I was awestruck by Henry's ability to move seamlessly from learning that market share had fallen the previous week (a downer), to greeting new employees (show time!), to meeting with powerful and unhappy distributors (absorb blows), to firing a senior executive (dish out the punishment) . . . all before lunch!

When you were in his presence, Henry made you feel like you were the only person in the world. Nothing was more important than his meeting with you, no matter what had just happened in his previous meeting or what might be coming next. I had never seen anything like this in academic life, where distractedness is an occupational hazard that gives rise to the stereotype of "the absent-minded professor."

When it came to a daily demonstration of ability, strength, and character, Henry gave a virtuoso performance every single day at work. Imitation is the sincerest form of flattery, and to this day I strive to emulate Henry's behavioral repertoire, emotional strength and steadiness, and his enveloping aura. Every once in a while, when someone compliments me on one of these characteristics, I feel like I've won an Olympic event.

This is the effect that the very best leaders have on those around them. They teach others to lead by who they are, what they do, and how they do it more than by what they say.

What successful Reptiles, Mammals, and Great Leaders share is high achievement. But Great Leaders represent a synergy of the best Reptilian and Mammalian characteristics, and then they add more: the ability to make change. Look at the descriptive words in the next table and you'll see what I mean: a Great Leader combines the toughness of a Reptile with the nurturing of a Mammal, adding vision and risk taking to achieve positive, consequential change.

It's fun to challenge yourself to come up with examples of well-known leaders who fall into each of these categories. For example, if I say Reptile, you might say Donald Rumsfeld or "Chainsaw Al" Dunlap (the former CEO of Scott Paper, whose autobiography was titled *Mean Business*—he got his nickname for firing

Reptile Leaders	Mammal Leaders	Great Leaders
Tough	Nurturing	Visionary
Aggressive	Cooperative	Inspiring
Analytical	Accommodating	Risk Taking
Detached	Engaged	Versatile
Competitors	Mensches	Giants
Deal Makers	Mentors	Builders
Survivors	Teachers	Legends

thousands of employees). If I say Mammal, you might say Mother Teresa or Jimmy Carter or the Dalai Lama. If I say Great Leader, you might say Steve Jobs or Colin Powell or Oprah Winfrey. We surely wouldn't always agree, and that's when it really gets interesting!

FOUNDATION REQUIREMENTS

We will investigate Reptiles, Mammals, and Great Leaders in depth in subsequent chapters. Let's focus here on the foundation requirements of the Leadership Pyramid.

When I reflect on all the conversations I've had as an executive or a board member about the suitability of candidates for a leadership appointment, or about a leader's performance and problems, I can fit *every issue* that has ever come up into one of the three foundation requirements: ability, strength, and character.

• *Ability.* Does the person have the requisite intelligence, knowledge, experience, or personal capacity (intellectual, emotional, and physical) to succeed on the job? You don't have to be the smartest person in the world to lead, but you have to be smart enough. You don't have to be an emotional rock, but you need to be centered most of the time and you need to be resilient and steady. Physical stamina is perhaps the least understood aspect of being a leader. Leadership is like a marathon. It definitely helps to have a good constitution and keep in good shape.

This book is mainly devoted to the abilities required for leadership excellence. I will have much more to say about the "ability" foundation requirements in the next several chapters.

• *Strength.* Does the person have the drive and determination, competitive spirit, sense of urgency, and ability to command the respect of others to succeed on the job?

Here's a simple proposition. Without strength, you can't lead. By strength, I mean drive, forcefulness, determination, the ability to exercise power, the need to achieve, and the desire to win. A person with ability but not strength is miserable in a leadership role.

Let me give you an example: There was a fellow in marketing at Cummins Engine Company we ended up firing. He'd been an able individual contributor, handling several accounts. Based on this performance, he was promoted to a job supervising a small group of people.

From the beginning, management was disappointed in his performance. He got feedback, he made promises, but performance was weak and there was little change. So we let him go.

When he cleaned out his desk, he brought me a big pile of letters, phone messages, to-do lists, and handwritten notes. "Here," he said, "these are from my 'too hard' drawer." "What do you mean?" I asked. He replied, "When I got into this job, people started bringing problems to me. You know, customer complaints, product problems, personnel stuff. I tried to deal with them. But after awhile it was too hard to deal with it all . . . so I just put it all in a drawer. I call it my 'too hard' drawer."

I've had to fire a lot of people over the years. It's my least favorite part of management work, but it's necessary and I've always felt that I owe it to people to do it clearly, cleanly, fairly, and personally. I've been struck by how often a person being fired for poor performance greets the news with relief. That was the case with the fellow with the "too hard" drawer. By the way, I've never met a leader who fired someone for poor performance who hasn't said, "In retrospect, I wish I'd done it sooner."

• *Character.* Does the person have the integrity, values, reliability, trustworthiness, loyalty, and independence required to succeed on the job?

J. Irwin Miller, founding father of Cummins Engine,

once told me: "When it comes to leadership, integrity and character count over specific skills every time." The reason is simple. In adults, integrity and character are largely determined and immutable, whereas skills and abilities can be developed. So the first filter in deciding who to appoint to a leadership role must be: Is this a person of good character and high integrity to whom I am willing to entrust others?

Irwin wasn't alone in this view. Leadership researchers asked more than 20,000 people around the world: "What characteristics do you look for and admire in your superiors?" The top four responses: honest, forward-looking, inspiring, and competent.[1]

Trust in one's supervisor also correlates with a range of positive leadership outcomes, including improved performance, job satisfaction, and organizational commitment.[2]

Most leaders are people of reasonably good character. But there is a special category of leader that deserves special attention: the few who are truly evil.

The dark side of character is malevolent leaders. These are people in positions of authority and power who are evil in what they do and how they do it. We are morbidly fascinated by the worst of them: Adolf Hitler, Jim Jones, Saddam Hussein come to mind. Bosses that fit this mold are the tyrants, sadists, and grossly insensitive boors who enjoy, or at least don't mind, making our lives miserable. Many believe in trying to lead through fear and intimidation. This is a strategy that works only with the weak and insecure, their favorite kind of subordinates. Evil leaders throw their weight around. They hurl insults and, whenever possible, humiliate people publicly rather than privately.

Like the Husseins and Hitlers of the world, they are usually bullies who, when stripped of the power of their leadership roles, are unimpressive and even pathetic. Who will ever forget, for example, the image of the once mighty Saddam Hussein, a man who sent over a million soldiers to their deaths in battle, meekly submitting to medical inspection by a U.S. army officer after surrendering without a struggle from the bottom of his hidey-hole?

Fortunately, evil leaders and their small-time brethren are not the subject of this book. But they do fit the framework presented here. Combine malevolence with perverted Reptilian characteristics and you get the monsters, tyrants, and thugs of the world. Combine malevolence with perverted Mammalian characteristics and you get manipulators, backstabbers, and Svengalis.

Setting aside evil leaders, the most important character challenge that leaders face is in the area of *integrity*. Let me explain.

HIGH-INTEGRITY LEADERSHIP

I believe that the foundation, the cornerstone, of excellent leadership is *high integrity*. In this regard, many leaders—from Richard Nixon (Watergate) to Martha Stewart (lying about insider trading), and Dennis Kozlowski (looting Tyco)—have been found wanting in recent years. What a disappointment.

There is a clear alternative. It is to commit yourself to being a high-integrity leader.

How? Let me keep it simple. It means that for your entire career:

- You will never knowingly violate just laws and regulations in any consequential way.

- You will be honest (i.e., tell the truth and not mislead).

- You will make commitments carefully and keep them faithfully.

- You will avoid conflicts of interest and when they are unavoidable, resolve them in favor of your duties and responsibilities, rather than benefiting yourself.

Perhaps this formula for high-integrity leadership seems too simplistic. I don't think so. Don't miss the abundant lessons from recent corporate scandals about how many senior executives failed to live up to these straightforward but challenging principles. Perhaps their thinking about integrity wasn't *simple enough*.

Didn't Richard Nixon listen when his mother told him, "Oh what a tangled web we weave, when first we practice to deceive?" Didn't the CEO of Adelphia remember that public companies are subject to laws and regulations intended to protect the interests of shareholders who have entrusted their savings to management? Didn't stockbrokers who churned their clients' accounts remember that they had promised to help those same clients save for their children's college educations or for a comfortable retirement?

As I reflect on these people who let themselves and others down, I think of my dad, who is ninety years old. He often told me as I grew up that one of the most important things in life is to be able to look yourself in the mirror in the morning without flinching. Good advice!

Perhaps the most difficult of the principles of high-integrity leadership is the fourth: to avoid conflicts of interest and when they are not avoidable, to resolve them in favor of your duties and responsibilities, not yourself. Why? If I were to cite a single, overarching transgression of leadership scandals in the political, nonprofit, and corporate worlds, it would be financial conflicts of interest. Time and again, people have done exactly the wrong thing. They capitalized on these conflicts for personal gain.

Conflicts of interest are abundant in professional life and especially in leadership work. With responsibility and power come privilege, access . . . and temptation. This is where being a high-integrity leader becomes a tremendous personal challenge.

Let me speak very personally on this matter.

In the 1990s, I was dean of the University of Michigan Business School. My team and I raised a lot of money—over $100 million—from individual donors for scholarships, professorships, institutes, and centers. And for a new $20 million building that we called Sam Wyly Hall.

Sam Wyly is a graduate of the University of Michigan Business School and an archetypal Texas entrepreneur. He has been the chairman of several public companies, including Michaels Stores. At the time I approached him for a $10 million gift to fund a new building on the business school campus, he was chairman of, and a big shareholder in, a public company called Sterling Software.

As Sam and I got acquainted in the course of numerous conversations about my gift request, his trust and confidence in me seemed to grow. I was ecstatic when he made an oral commitment to the $10 million gift for the building that would bear his name. Several weeks after Sam made that commitment, but before the commitment was paid or even formalized in writing, I received a call from him inviting me, on behalf of the board of Sterling Software, to become a director of the company.

It was an attractive opportunity. The tech sector was soaring in the late 1990s. Sterling was the world's fifth largest software company and highly profitable. Directors received a $50,000 a year fee and, more important, an initial grant of 50,000 options on Sterling stock that was, as I recall, selling at about $50 a share. You didn't have to be very good at math to calculate that if Sterling stock doubled—and in the tech boom that was the least one would expect—those options would be worth $2.5 million.

I was intrigued. I liked Sam and respected his business achievements. I did extensive due diligence on Sterling Software, and some of the smartest people I knew on Wall Street told me it was a solid company with good prospects. I was in an expensive time of life, with kids in college and graduate school, and I was saving for retirement. It also seemed to me that it would be awkward to say "no" to Sam at such a critical moment in the gift process.

So I agreed to join the board. But then I couldn't get comfortable with the decision and I wasn't sure why—until I attended my first meeting. What I realized as I sat at the board table was that I could not serve effectively as an independent director—speaking my mind, calling them as I saw them, and challenging Sam if and when required—with this major gift pending. And, at the same time, I was stricken with a concern that Sam's tremendous act of generosity—a $10 million gift to the University of Michigan—might be construed by some—and therefore tainted—as a *quid pro quo* for my support on the board, despite my official status as an independent director.

It was a classic conflict of interest. Where did my allegiances lie? As I sorted it out, the answer became obvious, as did the action I had to take. My first allegiance was to the University of Michigan, my employer, where I was a dean and faculty member. My second allegiance was to Sam Wyly as an alumnus and donor. My own interest in being a Sterling director and getting the fee and the rich option package had to come third. And, I concluded, my interest was incompatible with my allegiance to the university and to Sam as a donor.

So, immediately after that first board meeting, I met privately with Sam, explained my thinking to him, and resigned from the board. I felt a mixture of relief and a little regret when Sam said that he understood completely, respected my judgment on the matter, and accepted my resignation. The big option grant, of course, evaporated with the resignation.

Being human, I couldn't help tracking the price of Sterling Software stock for a while. It soared and the company was ultimately sold to Computer Associates for a big price. So my decision cost me a lot of money.

But it was the right thing to do and I would do it again today, faced with the same circumstances. A clear conscience is, truly, priceless.

Over the long haul, your most precious assets are your integrity, independence, reputation, and peace of mind. Always maintain and enhance them. The moral authority that comes with a clear conscience and taking the high road will strengthen your leadership effectiveness.

In this chapter we have covered the Foundation Requirements of the Leadership Pyramid: ability, strength, and character. In the next two chapters, we will learn what it means to achieve Reptilian and Mammalian excellence.

**Great
Leader
Requirements**
Innovative
Risk Taking
Appetite for Talent
Helicopter View
Sparkle Factor

**Reptilian
Requirements**
"Cold-Blooded"
Disciplined
Economic Sense
Financial Management
Verify, Control
Follow Up
Attention to Detail
Cool, Detached
Analytical

**Mammalian
Requirements**
"Warm-Blooded"
Nurturing
People Sense
Communications Ability
Trust, Delegate
Empower
Attention to Context
Warm, Engaged
Developmental

Foundation Requirements
Desire to be in Charge
Ability, Strength, Character

CHAPTER

Reptilian Excellence

L eaders need to be tough and tough-minded, at
times thick-skinned and even cold-blooded.

If I had to choose between working in an organization headed by a wimp or an S.O.B., I'd choose
the latter every time. In a competitive and unforgiving
world, a tough leader would give us a chance to survive. An organization with a weak leader is doomed to
failure.

In my experience, few things frustrate people more
than to be put in the charge of a person who is weak
and indecisive. It frightens them. We human beings
may not be as blatant about our expectations of hierarchical order as wolves (who is the leader of the pack?)

or birds (what is the pecking order?), but we want to know who is in charge and have confidence in that person's ability to lead us successfully.

Leaders not only need to *be* tough. They need to visibly *demonstrate* that they are tough from time to time. Showing physical toughness is a primitive and effective means of doing so. For example, Ronald Reagan's courageous and good-humored recovery from a failed assassination attempt raised his stock with Americans and strengthened his political hand. Rudolph Guiliani's personal bravery on 9/11 vaulted him into the national political spotlight.

Few fathers of adolescent sons escape those tumultuous years without an occasional physical showdown to maintain order in the family hierarchy. I have a brother-in-law who recalls vividly challenging his father to a fight when he was twelve, confident that he could take him. "I still can't believe how strong my dad was!" he reports fifty years later. Physical dominance creates a lasting impression. The velvet glove of international diplomacy depends from time to time on the iron hand of military power with its potential to conquer territory and physically dominate an adversary.

Demonstrations of leadership toughness in today's workplace seldom involve physical showdowns. So while this form of toughness is less important for leaders than it used to be (though not always unimportant—in negotiations, for instance, you don't want to be the first one to leave for a restroom break!), other forms of toughness are more important. They include *mental toughness, managerial toughness,* and *emotional toughness,* subjects I will discuss in this chapter.

This information will enable you to understand and act on answers to the following questions:

- Why do leaders need to be tough?

- What does it mean to be a tough leader?

- What capabilities and instincts do you need to develop in order to be a tough leader?

In short, this chapter will describe and help you develop what I call "Reptilian excellence," an essential requirement for strong, successful leadership.

WHY DO LEADERS NEED TO BE TOUGH?

There are at least five answers to that question. Leaders need to be tough to survive, to set the tone at the top, to establish authority and credibility, to get things done, and to ensure strong management.

Toughness Gives Their Organizations a Chance to Survive

Leaders need to be tough because they are responsible for companies and organizations that must survive in a competitive environment. For exactly this reason, in nature there are well-established protocols within many animal groups to ensure that the most dominant creature, the one who has initiated and survived challenges to the established order through various displays of toughness, is the leader. This selection process is vital to enhancing the survivability of the group.

Naturally Tough Leadership

The gorilla is the largest primate on earth. An adult male can be nearly six feet tall with a fingertip-to-fingertip wingspan approaching nine feet. The fully mature male has a light "saddle" of nearly white fur that runs down his back, side, and flank, and is hence called a silverback. There is a clear hierarchy based on size, and only the dominant silverback male breeds. As the center of attention, he leads his family group, deciding where they feed and sleep.

When a male gorilla meets a strange male, he will mount an elaborate threat display. It begins with hoots as he works himself into a frenzy and raises himself to full height, tearing at vegetation and pounding his chest with cupped hands. An ear-splitting roar precedes a few steps taken toward the intruder. If this fails, he goes into a full charge, screaming and waving his arms. But he usually stops short of actual contact and thrusts his face forward, so he's nose-to-nose with the intruder, staring, until one or the other backs down.

The challenge of survival in a threatening environment faces all organizations, even the largest and apparently strongest. Of the companies in the Fortune 500 in 2004, only seventy-one were on the initial list in the early 1950s. Beyond the private sector, which is a hotbed of "creative destruction," few organizations other than a handful of universities, the New York Stock Exchange, and the Catholic Church have managed to survive more than a century.[1]

Only the most senior leaders live every day with the threat of failure, severe contraction, or even extinction of their organizations. I remember walking through the main diesel engine assembly plant of Cummins Engine Company in Columbus, Indiana, with Irwin Miller. At the time, we were building nearly 500 heavy-duty engines in that factory every day, most of which were destined to power big rigs on North American highways. They generated $6 million a day in revenue for the company. People in southern Indiana, including our own employees, viewed Cummins as big, powerful, and permanent. Irwin's view was different. "Sometimes I'm amazed," he said, "at all the orders we get for these engines, and I think about how quickly they could dry up." This is a healthy attitude for a leader, since success can be—and often is—fleeting. Witness, for example, the stunning decline of GM and Ford.

Even in monopolistic and entrenched public-sector organizations, such as local school systems and great public universities, leaders must be concerned about decline, loss of public support and resources, and new forms of competition. I was a dean at the University of Michigan when online learning began to show up on our radar screens. It was about the same time that for-profit higher education also began to appear. I remember the reflexive, dismissive reaction of many of my colleagues: "Poor quality," "flash in the pan," "irrelevant," they said. Fifteen years later, online education serves millions of students. The for-profit University of Phoenix, which is the nation's largest private university, serves several hundred thousand students, many of them online. The fact is that no organization is immune from the threat of extinction or irrelevance. Traditional competitors should never be counted out and new forms of competition should never be dismissed. As Andy Grove of Intel Corp. has reminded us, when it comes to competition, "only the paranoid survive!"

Toughness Sets the Tone at the Top

While at the University of Michigan, I was once a coinvestigator in a massive study, sponsored by the Financial Executives Research Foundation, on internal control in U.S. companies. Long before the spectacular and well-publicized control failures at companies like Enron, Tyco, and WorldCom, we reported that one factor dominated in determining the effectiveness of internal control in organizations. We called it "tone at the top." People *must* know that their leaders expect and will hold them accountable for adherence to high standards of integrity and established policies and procedures, or else suffer the consequences for failure to do so.

Every leader faces moments of truth on this matter of imposing consequences. In those moments, toughness is required. One of mine came while I was dean of the University of Michigan Business School. On a Sunday afternoon, I received a call at home from a distraught mother of an undergraduate student. She asked if she and her daughter could see me right away. I said of course, drove to the office, and met for a couple of hours with mother and daughter.

They told me a sordid tale in which a highly regarded and high-performing member of our community violated a well-accepted standard, if not a formal policy, concerning relationships with undergraduate students. The next day, I brought in the employee and confronted him with the story. He denied it. I pressed hard and he eventually broke down, admitted the action, expressed great regret, and pleaded for mercy. It seems obvious now, in retrospect, that expelling him from our community was the right and necessary thing to do. But I found myself thinking, as leaders often do at such times, about his great performance, his contributions to our school, the lost talent his departure would represent, second chances, etc. For about a minute I deliberated the circumstances. Then I fired him.

When it comes to standards, accountability, and consequences, leaders must say what they mean and show they mean what they say. Actions that back up words—more than the words—determine a community's standards.

Toughness Establishes and Maintains Authority and Credibility

When ambitious people dream of being in a great leadership role—president, managing director, admiral, dean—they often think their quest will have ended when they get appointed or elected. Actually, their work has just begun.

The reason is that a certain amount of authority or formal power accompanies every job. But that authority has no value if the leader is not willing to exercise it. A leader must be prepared to use power—not ruth-

lessly, but confidently—to maintain authority and ensure credibility.

When I left the faculty to become a corporate executive, a colleague who was an expert on management
said to me, "Do you think you'll be able to exercise
power without excessive guilt?" At the time, I thought
it was a very odd question, but over the years I discovered it was a very good question. When, as a leader,
you occasionally have to disappoint people, extinguish
their professional dreams, or fire them, there is plenty
of potential for guilt that can be incapacitating in the
exercise of power. And a leader unwilling to exercise
power is destined to fail.

In retrospect, however, I think there was an even
better question my colleague could have asked me.
That is: "Do you think you'll be able to exercise power
without excessive *or inadequate* guilt?" Over the years
I've met a few leaders who really enjoy imposing pain
on others. They're scary, miniature versions of the
world's monsters and madmen.

Toughness Gets Things Done

Setting deadlines, being insistent, not taking no for an
answer, and demanding disciplined execution are all
essential for a leader to get things done, and done well,
through other people. I have been amazed at how stub-
born and single-minded the best leaders usually are.
How many times have we hoped the boss would forget
some harebrained (at least in our opinion) scheme he
came up with, only to have him bring it up six months
later and ask if we've accomplished it yet?

I learned a good lesson about setting deadlines when Cummins Engine built a new corporate headquarters in Columbus, Indiana. It was a Kevin Roche–designed building right in the center of town, and like all headquarters, it would say through its architecture, design, and execution a lot about our values and standards as a company. The project was proceeding at a snail's pace when one day Henry Schacht, the CEO, simply announced that he and the rest of the headquarters staff would be vacating their current offices and moving into the new building on an impossibly soon date. And we did. Of course, on move-in morning, we had to be awfully careful not to touch the final coats of paint that had been applied only hours before our arrival!

Another form of toughness is persistence. I read one time that persistence is the most underestimated of all corporate strategies. It's true of leadership strategies, too, especially when it comes to leading change. Here's an example.

I decided early in my tenure as dean at Michigan that we should add some practical, real-world, hands-on experience to the conceptual and analytical classroom education our students were getting. I told our faculty that it made no more sense to graduate our students without guided practical experience than it would for a medical school to graduate doctors who had not made rounds and done procedures under the guidance of experienced physicians.

There was a lot of faculty resistance to making this change. I'm sure many of the professors saw this as *my* hare-brained scheme and hoped I would forget about it! But I refused to go down in defeat. Instead, I stayed the course but came up with a different tactic. "Look," I said, "let's 'pilot' this change. We'll just try it." Using a pilot approach, we undertook "action learning" on a small scale. Within a year, the faculty voted to make action learning a requirement in our MBA program. Today, a dozen years later, under the leadership of my successor, it is a core competence and important point of competitive differentiation of the University of Michigan Business School ("Leadership in Thought and Action" is the school's tagline). Persistence is an important form of toughness. Leavened in this case with a little creativity and flexibility, it paid off in a major and lasting educational innovation.

Toughness Ensures Strong Management, Which Is Just as Important as Inspired Leadership

Tough-minded, demanding management, even perfectionism, is essential to successful leadership and is characteristic of high-performing organizations. Even small things matter in communicating standards and setting a tone. In my experience, many leaders fail simply because they can't make and meet budgets, they let people get away with murder, they tolerate sloppy housekeeping, and they can't make the trains run on time.

When Lou Gerstner took over as CEO of a mightily struggling IBM Corporation, he horrified the journalistic and business guru community by stating that IBM didn't need a vision at that moment; it needed better execution. Under his leadership, he achieved improved execution, which gave way later to a new vision and a totally revitalized company. A decade later, Larry Bossidy's book, *Execution* (Crown Business, 2002), a tome devoted to the subject of disciplined management versus strategic brilliance, became a business best-seller.

When I was dean, people noticed that I couldn't walk the hallways of my school without picking up random pieces of paper off the floor, including dirty tissues, and tossing them into wastebaskets. To me, this was both a matter of pride in our facilities and leading by example.

A decade earlier, Henry Schacht told me in my first month on the job at Cummins that he and I were going to take a "captain's tour" of the corporate headquarters (Henry was a former U.S. Navy officer). I couldn't believe it. The CEO walked me through the building and noted various problems for me to follow up on: leaves that had accumulated in the front entryway, floors that were dirty, walls that needed touch-up paint. And, as we walked, he scooped up off the floor every stray piece of paper we encountered! It didn't seem to bother Henry at all that responsibility for facilities wasn't part of my job. It dawned on me later that in his mind, it *was* my responsibility: mine, his, and all the other leaders of the company.

If you don't find this high-minded rationale for being tough-minded and detail-oriented compelling enough, let me offer you one other powerful inducement: avoiding embarrassment. I speak from experience.

Early in my tenure as dean, my office sent out a

printed invitation to an event. The invitation noted, "Public invited." Except that my staff had left out the "l" in public. I caught it right after the invitations went in the mail. That very day we instituted final quality checks on every single document that went out from my office, and we stuck with them for a decade, to great advantage. It was the kind of mistake you don't forget!

WHAT IT MEANS TO BE A TOUGH LEADER

Tough leadership comes in three dimensions: mental, emotional, and managerial.

Being a tough leader means being *mentally tough*. It means being passionate about achievement and winning, though not at any cost. It means seeing the world as it is, rather than as you want it to be or wish that it were. It means valuing facts and the people who deliver them, no matter how unpleasant the message. For leaders, *facts are friendly*.

Being a tough leader means being analytical. It means being realistic, neither excessively optimistic nor pessimistic, cynical or naïve.

An important part of mental toughness for leaders is being economically rational and financially literate. I'll have more to say about this later.

Tough leadership means being *emotionally tough*—steady, steely, resolute, relentless—without losing your humanity. It means being decisive and acting on your convictions, even if it means deciding not to act. It means caring about other people's respect for you but not so much about popularity.

Sometimes being emotionally tough just means carrying on and fulfilling your duties, obligations, and commitments even when you really don't feel like it, which is surprisingly often for many leaders.

With regard to the last point, I love the movie *All That Jazz,* which recounts the life and times of Bob Fosse, the brilliant choreographer. Fosse led a hard-driving work life by day and a wild and licentious, even debauched, personal life by night, frequently all night. In the film, Fosse (played by Roy Scheider) peers each morning into the bathroom mirror at his reddened eyes while nursing his hammering head. Watching him, you just know that he really, really wants to go back to bed. Instead, he concludes his ablutions by putting a determined smile on his face, cocking his head, and saying to his image, *"Showtime!"*

I told this story to each of three senior associate deans who were my leadership partners during a decade at the University of Michigan Business School. "Showtime" became our favorite code word for putting on our game faces and doing what had to be done, whether we felt like it or not. That's leadership. Every day is showtime.

Being a tough leader means being *managerially tough,* for example:

- Paying close attention all the time to the big picture and the details, to the clients and customers and your people, spotting needs and risks, problems and opportunities, achievements and failures, and making sure they're addressed, handled, and recognized

- Making economically sensible decisions and being on top of the numbers

- Having a plan and seeing to its disciplined execution

- Measuring performance, including your own, on results, not intentions

- Exercising strong, competent management of resources and ensuring effective control

- Saying "No!" when required and saying it directly, clearly, firmly, and unambiguously

The matter of saying "No!" deserves a comment. Irwin Miller once told me that the two hardest things for young managers to learn to say are "No!" and "I don't know." He was right, and they are good things to learn to say because they are straight, simple, direct, unadorned phrases. But sometimes there's a creative way to say no.

A friend of mine at Ford Motor Company told me this story about Red Poling, Ford's CEO at the time, a tough executive and a great golfer. According to the story, Poling met with Jack Nicklaus to discuss a golf course development on Ford land. He specified early on that the construction budget for the project was $2.5 million, period. Nicklaus patiently explained that a good course could only be built for about $200,000 per hole. "Fine," said Poling, "Then we're going to have the best damned twelve-hole course you've ever seen!"

Being Mentally Tough: Beware the Asch Effect

More than fifty years ago, social psychologist Solomon Asch conducted a series of laboratory experiments that shockingly demonstrated the power of peer pressure. Under the guise of a "perception test," volunteer groups of college students looked at twelve pairs of cards like the ones shown below. The object was to identify the line that was the same length as the standard line. Each individual was told to announce his choice to the group. Since the difference among the comparison lines was obvious, there should have been unanimous agreement on every card. But that was not the case.

Standard Line Card   Comparison Line Card

All but one member of every group were Asch's confederates—secretly placed to systematically select the wrong line. The remaining individual was the naïve subject who was being tricked. Group pressure was created by having the naïve subject be among the last to announce his choice.

So how often did the naïve subject conform to a majority opinion that was obviously wrong? Only 20 percent of Asch's subjects remained entirely independent; 80 percent yielded to the pressures of group opinion at least once, and 58 percent buckled under the obviously incorrect majority at least twice.[2]

Leadership Lesson: Be wary! A unanimous, incorrect opposition can distort your judgment.

WHAT ARE THE CAPABILITIES AND INSTINCTS TO DEVELOP TO BECOME A TOUGH LEADER?

A famous saying commonly heard among poker players, is that "You've got to know when to hold them, know when to fold them." As a leader, you need to know when to be tough and when to be warm, empathetic, and understanding.

In my experience, leaders must display exceptional toughness in six areas:

1. Understanding financial matters

2. Setting the bar high

3. Dealing with bullies

4. Serving as judge and jury

5. Cutting

6. Litigating

In these matters, a reputation for being "smart, tough, and fair" is the proper aspiration for an excellent leader.

Understanding and Handling Financial Matters

Being grounded in economics is essential for leaders. Consider the practical consequences for leaders of understanding comparative advantage, supply and demand, price mechanisms, incentives, sunk costs, and unintended consequences, as well as monetary and fiscal policy, financial markets, and international matters like exchange rates, balance of trade, and stages of economic growth. Such understanding not only helps leaders make good decisions. It enables them to tune out the noise, garbage, and hysteria that clutter the airwaves and print media under the heading of business and economic news.

No need, for example, to listen ever again to explanations of daily movements of the stock market. No need to lose sleep over the total demise of Social Security in our and our children's lifetimes—it's not going away. No need to worry about hurting your broker's feelings if you move your money into low-cost, no-load index funds—he's your broker, not your friend.

Accordingly, there are two academic courses no aspiring leader should miss: Economics 101 and Basic Accounting.

Economics 101. No discipline makes a greater contribution to the tough-mindedness of leaders than economics. It cuts through the emotional fog that tends to envelop us as warm, sentient creatures, seriously impairing our objectivity, analytical capabilities, and decision making. As I noted previously, mental toughness requires leaders to see the world as it is. Economics really helps in this regard.

Let me illustrate. I have a colleague, a very smart woman of Singaporean birth, who excelled in school, earned her undergraduate degree at Cambridge (U.K.), was attracted to Marxism, and later decided to do a

Ph.D. in economics. The title of her doctoral dissertation was "Multinational Firms and Manufacturing for Export in Less-Developed Countries: The Case of the Electronics Industry in Malaysia and Singapore." Given her Marxist leanings, she approached her study with a strong point of view, or hypothesis, which was that multinational firms were seriously exploiting the female factory workers of Southeast Asia.

Good economic research is fact-based and data-driven, and my colleague is a good economist. In her fieldwork in Southeast Asia, she found something quite different than she had expected. Many of the female employees of the multinational firms reported to my colleague that while their working conditions were difficult, their "sweatshop" work represented a great improvement in their lives. They learned valuable skills. Their wages were far higher than what they had earned previously. Their pay was providing their families with a firm step up the economic ladder toward a better life. And so on.

My colleague's research turned up facts that she reported honestly. It also changed her mind substantially about business and its effects on people in developing countries. For her, facts were friendly, even though they were inconvenient, at least in the short term. This is what good economic analysis, combined with good fact-gathering and an open mind, can do: turn a preconception or conventional wisdom on its ear and enable you as a leader to see the world as it really is.

Twenty-five years after my colleague conducted her research and five years after she told me about it, I was interim president of the University of Michigan. When you sit in the president's office at such an institution, which has a great tradition of student activism, one of the things you have to get used to is student demonstrations for all kinds of causes. Some of those demonstrations come to call on you. Sometimes they're friendly, sometimes not.

One winter day in 2002, demonstrators for SOLE (Students Organizing for Labor and Economic Equality) paid me a visit. One of their concerns was sweatshop conditions for workers in developing countries who produced athletic apparel for suppliers to the University of Michigan. Another was the labor practices of a company in New York State that also produced such gear. Let me say that I am passionately opposed to illegal, unethical, and unsavory business practices, especially those that exploit people. I also have an enormous soft spot in my heart for students who champion the underdog, have a strong streak of idealism, and are prepared to take personal risks to create a better world. This describes most of the students in SOLE on our campus.

At the same time, I felt an obligation to confront the students with some of the hard economic consequences that might occur if the university used its muscle and overplayed its hand in trying to right purported wrongs. These would include loss of jobs and income for the people they wanted to help.

I won't claim to have changed minds on the spot. But I am confident that sharing my faculty colleague's story—and how her Marxist sympathies gave way in the face of facts to a more objective, balanced, and nuanced understanding of the same concerns—helped bridge what might have been a great gulf between us. I also believe that it contributed to the students' education (which, after all, is the mission of a university) in a more memorable fashion than a normal classroom discussion of international economics would have.

Basic Accounting. The language of business, and of every organization when it comes to money, is accounting. In this regard, we don't have the luxury of assuming what Americans do when they travel to a foreign country (i.e., that everyone will speak English). No, leaders need to learn the language of accounting.

Specifically, this means financial accounting (versus, say, cost accounting), which covers—at a minimum—three key financial statements: profit and loss (or revenue and expense), balance sheets, and cash flow. It's also important to understand budgets, both operating and capital, and how to evaluate results against plan and prior periods.

Accounting as practiced at the highest level, by auditors and chief accounting officers, involves a great deal of esoteric detail. Much of it is intellectually interesting but not crucial to a senior leader's understanding. One way to separate the wheat from the chaff is to become proficient at reading and picking out important issues from the footnotes to financial statements and from what is called the MD&A (Management Discussion and Analysis) that accompanies financial statements. Pay special attention to a section called Critical Accounting Estimates, since financial statements, counter to their appearance of high precision, are replete with estimates and are deeply affected by invisible things such as revenue recognition policies and depreciation schedules.

Focusing on three critical questions has helped keep me grounded in the face of financial reporting complexity. I attribute them to my father, for whom auditing is a calling akin to the priesthood (he's a CPA):

- What is happening to *cash flows* (versus reported profits, which are much more affected by estimates)?

- What are *actual to actual* (versus actual to plan or budget) results?

- What are results for *comparable operations* this period versus prior periods (what retailers call "same store" comparisons)?

If you can figure out *cash-in versus cash-out* for this period (year, quarter, month) versus last period for comparable operations, it will tell you a lot about the actual operating performance of the business.

Balance sheets can look complex, but at bottom they are very simple. They answer a fundamental question: How strong is this company financially? What are its assets, especially liquid and current assets (cash, receivables) versus its liabilities, especially short-term liabilities (accounts payable)? How much debt does it have and when is it due? What does the balance sheet tell me about how well the organization is positioned to weather bad times when net cash flow is weak or negative for a sustained period?

Finally, an understanding of accounting requires attention to a soft but vital matter: the quality of internal control in the organization. Without strong internal controls (e.g., financial and accounting policies and adherence to them, accuracy of accounting records, fraud avoidance and detection), *there is no reason to believe what the financial statements are reporting with apparent precision!* How else to explain companies like Enron, WorldCom, and Parmalat collapsing, virtually overnight, from a condition of robust health as reported in their financial statements? How good were controls (and audits) at Parmalat when a $10 billion account at Bank of America—an account that was included on audited, publicly reported balance sheets for years—proved to be *fictitious*?

Through attention and experience, leaders must develop an instinct about financial reports, which is simply: "Do the numbers make sense to me?" (I also attribute this question to my CPA father.) I had a very difficult experience as the director of F & M Distributors, Inc., a public company that ultimately went bankrupt, that illustrates the importance of the question.

F & M was a fast-growing retail company selling discount health and beauty aids. At each board meeting, management presented a rosy report on financial results, emphasizing top-line (revenue) growth as the key measure of success for a growing company. Profits were modest and cash flow was strained, which is not unusual in growing companies. But as I studied the financial statements, charted some trends, and did a back-of-the-envelope projection, it appeared to me that there was real cause for concern about the sustainability of the company's growth. Its slim profits, low cash balances, and substantial debt levels posed a threat to its long-term financial viability. It worried me a lot that as a board member (a part-time job) I seemed more concerned than management (full-timers!) about our trajectory and its consequences.

I asked a lot of questions, got what I viewed as inadequate answers, and clearly began to be viewed by management and my colleagues as a boardroom Cassandra. But after checking and rechecking my numbers, I made an appointment to see the chairman privately and told him that I believed we were on a path to eventual bankruptcy, even though it was not yet apparent. I told him that as far as I was concerned, management needed to do several things immediately, such as close money-losing stores, slow the rate of expansion, and conserve cash. If they didn't, I would have to resign from the board. Management didn't, I resigned, and eighteen months later the company filed for bankruptcy protection.

Moral of the story: The rosy numbers that were being reported in board meetings just didn't square with my analysis of the numbers, what I saw happening in the stores and warehouses, and my wife's and her friends' negative reports from their shopping experiences. *Something was wrong.* As a leader, you need to develop such instincts and trust them. It's imperative to wrestle your disquiet to the ground, in part by burying yourself, all alone, in the numbers.

It would be nice to conclude this story by reporting that I was a genius and came out smelling like a rose. Instead, I came out smelling like litigation, since securities lawsuits ensued after the company's bankruptcy declaration (as they nearly always do) and all directors, past and present, were swept into it. The case was ultimately settled, but it was a difficult and troubling experience.

Lesson: Leaders need to be on top of the numbers and the numbers must make sense!

Setting the Bar High and Making Sure It Doesn't Slip

Leaders are responsible for a work system and for the people in it. It's important to expect a lot from people, and it's fair to communicate those expectations in standards that reduce ambiguity without eliminating flexibility, initiative, and innovation, all of which are valuable. Knowing what is expected is something that people at work should be able to count on. It's the responsibility of leaders to supply the answer by defining and communicating clear performance standards.

People in many jobs do have clear performance standards. For example, salespeople have goals and quotas; attorneys track wins, losses, and settlements and generate billable hours; physicians in HMOs manage a defined patient population and have health outcomes and cost parameters to consider; professors teach a required number of credit hours; teachers are often measured on their students' performance on standardized tests; portfolio managers strive to achieve a total return better than the market and in the upper quartiles and deciles relative to their peers; CEOs strive to grow earnings and shareholder value at rates that exceed industry medians and means.

There's a saying in business that "what gets measured gets attention." A related concept is that what gets attention—and incentives—gets results. An important feature of Reptilian leadership is to be fanatical about measurement, especially in the area of performance standards for individuals, groups, units (divisions, departments, teams), and the whole organization.

Yes, it's true that excessive focus on measurable results can produce undesirable, unintentional consequences. Yes, it's true that there are vitally important areas of performance that don't easily lend themselves to measurement. Yes, it's true that it's a poor leader (and economist) who knows the price of everything and the value of nothing. But none of these important reminders takes away from the central fact that leaders must be crystal clear about what constitutes excellent performance. You must demand it, measure it, reward it, and take action if there are sustained performance shortfalls.

The quality movement in Japan, America, and around the world during the last thirty years has made an enormous contribution to "making the invisible visible," as the Japanese say, when it comes to performance standards. Gordon Food Service (GFS), an extraordinary, hundred-year-old, family-controlled private company headquartered in Grand Rapids, Michigan, has a quality program that serves as a good example. (Disclosure: I have been a GFS board member for eighteen years.) GFS is in a conceptually simple but operationally complex business. It purchases more than 10,000 different kinds of food items from manufacturers, receives and warehouses them, and sells and delivers them to thousands of restaurants, institutions, and other food service operations in the United States and from coast-to-coast in Canada.

GFS divisions report regularly on their financial results *and* their quality performance. The performance standards couldn't be clearer and they speak loudly to all of the employees, as well as to GFS customers and suppliers. Here is an example of results for a recent fiscal year:

Gordon Food Service
Quality Program
Full Year Results

Quality Area	Performance Goal	Actual Performance
% in Stock	98.90%	98.83%
Loads Departing on Time	98.80%	99.20%
Vehicle Safety	91.25%	90.49%
Employee Safety	95.60%	96.17%
Credits	0.70%	0.73%
Product Loss Preshipment	0.19%	0.19%
Employee Suggestions Handled	99.00%	91.00%
Vendor Involvement Program	100.00%	100.00%

Charts with quality goals and results such as these are widely displayed throughout the company. GFS is a good example of a company that defines performance standards clearly, measures them carefully, and shares them widely.

GFS also believes strongly in incentives and ties employee compensation and other rewards closely to company, team, and individual performance. Indeed, I have never encountered another company that lionizes high-performing individuals and teams like GFS. As a director, I've had the pleasure of joining great GFS transit drivers, salespeople, deliverymen, warehouse pickers, and Gordon family members at once-in-a-life-time events like the Summer Olympics in Atlanta or the Winter Olympics in Salt Lake City. This is one of Gordon's ways of thanking its outstanding employees (and their families) and celebrating their extraordinary work performance. If performance measures and in-centives are the Reptilian side of GFS, recognition of employees is the extraordinarily Mammalian side of the company.

Dealing with Bullies

I've found that 95 percent of the people one deals with as a leader are fine. They're normal human beings and more or less on the same page as you, despite occa-sional differences on substantive matters. But all lead-ers encounter a handful of people who are deeply neurotic. They don't play well with others, as my for-mer assistant liked to say. And many have a special problem with people who have authority over them (i.e., you). Maybe it's unresolved family problems or brain chemistry or who knows what, but as a leader, you don't really care why. What you know for sure is that these people are a problem.

Bullies are a special case of "problem people" leaders must engage with extreme toughness. Bullies are grown-up versions of the school playground variety, the ones who liked to terrorize nice kids, pick on weak kids, and generally throw their weight around to get their way. With bullies, your job is to defend less powerful people since bullies are not very brave and they tend to focus their attention on people they can cow.

Leaders must be tough in dealing with bullies because the only force that deters them is power, which you possess, and the only language they understand is action. They interpret talk as appeasement. They believe that genuine collaboration and compromise, versus the deceitful and temporary variety at which they excel, are for the weak. Bullies are a serious threat to the commonwealth of any organization. A hard but necessary lesson for successful leaders to learn is that you must deal with these people differently than most. With bullies, the leader's goal and strategy must be to prevail by using power and plenty of it.

Serving as Judge and Jury: Policy Violations and Integrity Infractions

Earlier in this chapter, I recounted an egregious example of an employee violating university standards, behaving without integrity, then lying to cover it up. I fired him. Most incidents of policy violation and infractions of integrity are not so dramatic, but the guiding principle for strong leaders is the same: Be tough, and make sure that the punishment is proportionate to the offense. Justice is important, but even more important is that by dealing with such infractions strongly and fairly, you prevent more infractions over the long term.

I have chaired and served on the audit committees of the boards of directors of several companies. Service on an audit committee exposes you to the seamier side of human behavior in organizations. At every meeting there is a report on cases of employee fraud that have been detected, investigated, and addressed. Although the number of such cases is quite small, the stream of them is endless. They stand as testimony to weakness in our human character. Most cases are acts of theft (of money and property) motivated by greed, designed with creativity, and covered up through dishonesty.

You might think that the consequences for individuals who perpetrate these acts are complex and varied, because the nature of their offenses vary. But the opposite is true. Virtually without exception, the employee is fired and in most instances prosecuted. Management and audit committees know they must back up policy with action and remind people that when they're caught, crime doesn't pay.

Sometimes it's worth taking hard action even if you can't make it stick. That's a surprising assertion since you might think that management credibility would suffer. Here's a case where it didn't.

At a company where I worked as an executive, we knew we had a drug dealer working out of his car in the parking lot of one of our facilities. Some of our employees complained about it repeatedly. But try as we might, we couldn't put together rock-solid evidence against the guy. Despite that, we convinced the local police of probable cause. The fellow was arrested but ultimately not prosecuted because of lack of evidence. However, two good things happened as a result. He went away. And our employees knew that we cared enough about their work environment and concerns to take action, even though we didn't prevail.

Cutting

My late friend Mike Walsh, who was CEO of Union Pacific Railroad and Tenneco Corporation, once said, "If you can't stand taking hard action, don't go into management. It's like choosing to be a surgeon when you can't stand the sight of blood."

It was a good analogy because both surgeons and managers have to do plenty of cutting. Surgeons cut tissue. Managers must, from time to time, cut budgets, jobs, suppliers, whole businesses, facilities, and operations. Because this leadership work is so difficult and emotionally charged, a euphemistic vocabulary has grown up around it. Companies "downsize," "right size," reduce, restructure, tighten up, and streamline. Call it what you will, it's all cutting.

Surgeons are the tough guys and gals of the medical world. Being tough in their specialty doesn't mean that surgeons can't have a pleasant bedside manner and be kind at home to their spouses, children, and dogs. But when the chips are down, we want our surgeons to be tough: professional, decisive, competent, and in charge in the operating room. This is exactly what a leader must be when engaged in the difficult but necessary work of cutting people and resources.

I feel like I've seen nearly every mistake leaders can make while cutting. I watched one manager do a Clint Eastwood tough-guy act leading up to the decision to cut, then delegate all the dirty work to the human resources department—the opposite of leading by example. I've seen managers so traumatized by having to deliver bad news to people that they walled off their emotions and became automatons until it was over. I participated in a management team that was overwhelmed with guilt and sorrow at the action we had to take. As a result, we approved a schedule of severance payments so generous that it actually prevented people from facing up to the vital need to start looking for work soon after losing their jobs, so that more than the usual number ended up lethargic, depressed, and ineffective.

I was close to a situation in which communications were so poor that an employee came out of a meeting with his supervisor thinking that he'd gotten a positive performance review when his supervisor's job was to fire him as part of a downsizing! This employee literally didn't know that he had been fired; I learned this when I had to set him straight about the message.

How could this happen, you ask? Easily. A flustered supervisor stumbles his way through the following sort of dialogue:

> "You know, Joe, you've been a great employee for a long time. We're really grateful for all you've done for the company. Everyone thinks the world of you

here. But we're going through hard times and everyone has to do his part. I'm sorry things aren't going
to work out as we planned, I'm really sorry. Well,
thanks, Joe, for all that you've done for the company.
You're a strong person and I know you'll be fine."

End of meeting. The supervisor thinks he delivered
the separation message; Joe thinks he received an odd
but positive review of his performance. Yes, it really
happens.

Strong and effective leadership in cutting requires
the surgical approach: professional, planned, decisive,
competent, and in charge. Because the patient is awake
and aware, though usually in a state of shock, there are
additional requirements. The leader should communicate honestly and openly that cuts are going to occur,
why they are occurring, who will be affected, and how
and when the actions will be taken. In delivering the
bad news, leaders should set the example by personally firing those on the cut list who report directly to
them and telling their subordinates personally about
required cuts in their operations and budgets.

The delivery of such news should be crystal clear,
succinctly delivered, and communicated in a way that
extends respect and dignity to the other person. The
leader must be emotionally strong, sympathetically observing anger (or shock or grief) but not succumbing to
or reciprocating it. Early in my career, I made the mistake of leaving a person crying in a room after I fired
him because I couldn't stand to be there. Word got
around the organization about what I had done and
that it was heartless, which it was. Since then, I sit,

wait, and offer a tissue until the tears have subsided and we can have a proper conclusion to the meeting.

In my experience, when you have to deliver bad news to people, they react poorly both to harshness and remoteness on the one hand, and sugarcoating (what Irwin Miller called "soft-soaping") or excessive sympathy on the other. What they appreciate is the truth, the facts, emotional strength, and being treated respectfully. In cutting, that's the right way to be a tough leader.

Litigating and Other Zero-Sum "Games"

Economists and behavioral scientists have recognized for years that there are two forms of "games" people play when resources are involved. One they call zero-sum: Resources are fixed and whatever I gain comes at your expense, and vice versa. The other they call mutual gain: The resource pie can expand if we cooperate or contract if we compete. There are ways of playing the game and outcomes that allow both of us to win—or lose.

Most of the time, good leaders figure out how to create mutual gain situations with their people. A good example is profit-sharing. If we all work together, do a good job, and increase the company's profit, we'll all get paid more through profit-sharing. And mutual gain doesn't always involve money. A lot of leadership involves understanding what various stakeholders—customers, employees, suppliers, owners—want and figuring out initiatives, programs, and deals that leave everyone better off.

When I was dean of the University of Michigan Business School, it was clear to me that everyone— faculty, students, staff, alumni, and my bosses in central administration—wanted the school's performance and reputation to strengthen and (let's admit it) its rankings to be high. My job was to urge faculty to do more and better research and be innovative in teaching and curriculum; raise money from alumni to support our cause; and engage students to help improve the school and, as a result, rate us highly in the periodic *Business Week* and other rankings surveys. It worked. All stakeholders did their parts; the school got better, and with it came recognition. We parlayed recognition into more resources and opportunities for everyone. It became a virtuous cycle.

It would be nice if leaders only had to play the "mutual gain" game. It's a great Mammal act! But they don't. Sometimes they have to play zero-sum games where there is a clear winner and a clear loser and the leader's responsibility is to win. This is a job for a Reptile.

It is extremely important for leaders to recognize the game in which they are engaged and to play accordingly. I used to get expressions of confusion from people who filed grievances against me or sued me. "I thought you said you wanted to problem-solve this, and now you say your goal is to prevail," they would squawk. "I *did* want to problem-solve it and I *would have* tried until the cows came home," I would reply. "But you chose to change the game when you filed that suit. Now we are in a formal dispute in which a third party is going to decide if I'm right or you're right.

That's completely different from working together to come up with a mutually satisfactory outcome. You chose this game, you're attacking me and I'm defending myself. Your goal is to win, and so is mine. We can't both win anymore."

As the Leadership Pyramid in Chapter 3 illustrates, leaders need to be highly versatile. Nowhere is this more important than when you are engaged in a disagreement with another party and you must make the conscious shift from *informal problem solving,* in which a Mammalian approach (i.e., listening, conciliation, and compromise) works best, to *a formal dispute resolution process,* such as grievances and litigation, in which a highly Reptilian approach (i.e., extreme toughness) is required.

We turn next to the challenge of developing Mammalian excellence.

**Great
Leader
Requirements**
Innovative
Risk Taking
Appetite for Talent
Helicopter View
Sparkle Factor

**Reptilian
Requirements**
"Cold-Blooded"
Disciplined
Economic Sense
Financial Management
Verify, Control
Follow Up
Attention to Detail
Cool, Detached
Analytical

**Mammalian
Requirements**
"Warm-Blooded"
Nurturing
People Sense
Communications Ability
Trust, Delegate
Empower
Attention to Context
Warm, Engaged
Developmental

Foundation Requirements
Desire to be in Charge
Ability, Strength, Character

CHAPTER 5

Mammalian Excellence

A
ddressing the University of Kansas in Lawrence on March 18, 1968, Robert F. Kennedy
said:

"The gross national product does not allow for the
health of our children, the quality of their education,
or the joy of their play. It does not include the beauty
of our poetry or the strength of our marriages; the
intelligence of our public debate or the integrity of
our public officials. It measures neither our wit nor
our courage; neither our wisdom nor our learning;
neither our compassion nor our devotion to our
country; it measures everything, in short, except that
which makes life worthwhile."

Kennedy's lament about the shortcomings of the GNP also applies to leadership that fails to move beyond the Reptilian. Reptilian competence is a necessary but not sufficient condition for leadership excellence. Reptilian leaders can enable their organizations to survive. Only Mammalian leaders can enable organizations and their members to thrive.

WHY DO LEADERS NEED TO NURTURE?

In Chapter 4, I described Reptilian excellence and discussed why leaders must be tough, what it means to be tough, and how to become a tough leader. In this chapter, I describe Mammalian excellence: why successful leaders must be nurturing and what it means to do a great job in the care, feeding, growth, and development of people.

I hope it was clear in the last chapter that being tough isn't being mean. I hope it will be clear in this chapter that being a nurturer doesn't mean being soft or sappy. Indeed, there is a simple, compelling, and hard-edged reason to be an intensely nurturing leader: It's the only way I know to develop great people who are the *sine qua non* of every high-performing organization. Contributing to the development of great people is highly rewarding for a nurturing leader!

For example, let me tell you about Allan Afuah, who was the most extraordinary young faculty member I met during a decade as dean at the University of Michigan. He was born in a tiny village in the African country of Cameroon where his parents still live. They speak a tribal language shared by only a few thousand people. Allan was educated by missionaries who spotted his academic ability and potential and urged him to seek a scholarship and go to college abroad. He graduated with a degree in engineering from the University of Oregon, then worked in the information industry in Silicon Valley, Austin, Texas, and Route 128 near Boston. Allan's intellectual curiosity and drive for achievement led him to the Massachusetts Institute of Technology (MIT) and the field of corporate strategy, where he earned his master's degree and Ph.D. His research was in Internet business models, a hot area at the time. In 1995 we recruited him to Michigan.

Allan faced the usual challenges in establishing himself as a faculty member: teaching, research and publishing, and service. Effort is crucial to early success and Allan was the hardest-working person on the faculty, bar none. I don't ever recall coming to the business school, day or night, weekday or weekend, vacation or holiday, when he wasn't in his office or at the library, toiling away. He proved to be a talented teacher and had no problem with service.

But in research, Allan marched to his own drummer. Conventional wisdom for rookies is simple and universal. Choose a narrow topic and publish modest but high-quality articles in top refereed journals. Be incremental: Accept your field as it is and advance it slightly through your work. Go for bunts and singles; don't swing for the fences until you're tenured and senior. Colleagues drummed this advice into Allan's head. He listened politely but he had a different plan.

I took a special interest in Allan because of his extraordinary promise, remarkable work ethic, and unique background. I, like his colleagues, made sure Allan knew the conventional wisdom on how to achieve early professional success in research. But I could see we weren't making a sale, so I asked Allan what he intended to do. His plan was simple and audacious: "I'm going to write a book to use in my course. Every chapter is going to be written as an article to be submitted for publication, and I'm going to do it all in less than a year."

Allan's colleagues were convinced that this was a sure-fire formula for failure. I thought they were probably right, but Allan's talent and determination made a big impression on me. It also occurred to me that Allan had already beaten far bigger odds in his life than those represented by the new professional bet he was making. Besides, I could see he was going to do it his way no matter what anyone told him. So I decided as dean to quietly and persistently encourage and support him in ways both tangible and intangible. I would stop by his office regularly to offer him words of encouragement.

Allan succeeded brilliantly. He wrote the book, he published articles out of it, and he did it in less than a year. The rest, as they say, is history. He has rocketed to academic success. What a joy this has been to behold!

Recently, Allan sent me his latest book, and I leafed through the first few pages. On the dedication page, I found a printed tribute:

> To my grandmother, Veronique Masang Nkweta, and
> to the Bamboutou highlands which she and my
> mother hoed to raise me.
>
>   Allan Afuah

On the same page, I also found a handwritten note that reminded me what a privilege it is to be in a position of leadership where you can nurture the growth and development of others:

Joe:

Thanks for creating an environment that allowed all of us to be the best that we can be. I am eternally grateful. This book would not be possible without your leadership at Michigan. Thanks!!!

Allan

POSITIVE ORGANIZATIONAL SCHOLARSHIP: THRIVING, NOT JUST SURVIVING

Have you ever been to a psychiatrist? If you to go to the psychiatric outpatient clinic at the University of Michigan Medical Center, the receptionist will hand you a bright orange piece of paper to give to your therapist during your session (it's bright orange because it triggers the billing procedure and the administrators don't want you or the doctor to forget it or lose it). On the front of that piece of paper is information about you and your health insurance, if you have it. But if you turn it over, you'll find something startling to us laypeople. It is column after column, in tiny type, of the possible maladies for which you might be seeking psychiatric assistance. This American Psychiatric Association (APA) classification sheet has something like 256 codes. Your therapist, after sizing you up, is supposed to check off the neuroses and psychoses she finds are plaguing you.

This is fine. But what is striking is the absence of categories like "doing well but wants to do better" or "has a good marriage but wants to make it deeper and richer" or "appears psychologically healthy but wishes to thrive," and so on. The emerging field of Positive Organizational Scholarship (POS) is dedicated to the organizational equivalents of these individual aspirations.

Kim Cameron, professor of organization and management at the University of Michigan Business School, and one of the founders of POS, describes the field as "the examination of extraordinarily positive dynamics in organizations and the factors that unleash the highest in human potential."

Cameron goes on to say that POS studies organizational characteristics like appreciation, collaboration, virtuousness, vitality, and meaningfulness in which "creating abundance and human well-being" are key indicators of success. Cameron and others examine organizational characteristics like trustworthiness, resilience, humility, authenticity, respect, and forgiveness among employees. Their research has led to theories of transcendence, positive deviance, extraordinary performance, and positive spirals of flourishing.

I imagine that at this point you might be rolling your eyes. But I've seen it work, so I know the aspiration can be realized. And what human being would not welcome the opportunity to be a member of an organization that could be so described?

I have actually had experience in organizations that fulfill this remarkable vision. It's true at Gordon Food Service. It's been true for years at Southwest Airlines, the only consistently successful competitor and profitable company in the U.S. airline industry over the last forty years. It's true at Focus: HOPE in Detroit, an inspiring nonprofit human services organization. It's true at a lot of organizations you've never heard of. And many people, like Allan Afuah, have told me it was true for them in the 1990s at the University of Michigan Business School when I was dean.

So I know that POS's impossible dream is, in fact, possible. Because it's possible and desirable to have organizations that are *both* high performing and highly nurturing, why should we ever again settle for anything less? Answer: We shouldn't.

Positive Organizational Scholarship reminds me of a professional visit I made to the Mayo Clinic twenty years ago. A physician leader described the clinic's allocation of square footage to make an important point. He said, "Ninety-five percent of our space is devoted to illness: diagnosing and treating sickness of all kinds. Five percent is devoted to prevention: figuring out what being well means, helping people stay that way, and improving on already good health."

What is my point? It is to remember that the goal of the best leaders is to create the conditions to enable people and organizations to grow, develop, and thrive, not just survive. That's what Mammalian excellence is all about.

WHAT IT MEANS TO BE
A NURTURING LEADER

Achieving Mammalian excellence requires three leadership attitudes and practices:

- Treat people with dignity and respect.

- See and develop the potential in people.

- Make it about your people, not about you.

Afraid of Burning Out?

An in-depth longitudinal study on "professional burnout" discovered that antidotes include 1) active interest of the boss, 2) finding greater autonomy and support, and 3) finding meaningful work.[1] All things a good Mammalian leader provides.

Treat People with Dignity and Respect

Every day, in every interaction, as a leader you have a choice regarding how to treat people. You can bully and belittle them; you can be self-absorbed, remote, and distracted; or you can choose to focus on people, affirming their dignity and extending respect in ways small and large, verbal and nonverbal, tangible and intangible.

As a leader, I have been stunned both by the number of opportunities to do the right thing in this regard and by virtually everyone's deep desire to be treated with dignity and respect by people in positions of authority. Some people wear this need on their sleeves. Others cover it up with denial and disdain for those in charge.

In either case, leaders should take special care to extend dignity and respect to all people. I held an all-employee meeting for members of my department a few months after joining Cummins Engine Company. We went into a question-and-answer session following my formal remarks. A woman at the back of the room raised her hand. I can remember what she said like it was yesterday. "Mr. White, I'm only an hourly person but . . ." She went on to ask her question, but I never heard it. I was lingering on those words *"I'm only an hourly person."* I was struck by the self-denigration rooted in a label ("hourly") established by wage-and-hour laws simply to ensure that people without a salary will earn overtime pay when they put in more hours than a normal workday or workweek!

My response to her came straight from the gut, not the brain: "I don't care if you are an hourly person or salaried, exempt or nonexempt, a college graduate or without a formal education, a man or a woman, black, white, or anything else. We're all people working together. And you never have to apologize for who you are." Then I asked her to repeat her question and I answered it.

Why was my reaction so strong? I don't know for sure. But I suspect it had something to do with my love of and admiration for my grandfathers who were, on my mother's side, an Italian immigrant who painted gasoline pumps in the Bennett Pump factory in Muskegon, Michigan, and on my father's side, a cook from a large family in Virginia. A great thing about American society is that few of us are very far from humble origins, so it's not hard to put ourselves in the shoes of people on other rungs of the economic ladder.

There is another reason that leaders should take special care to extend dignity and respect to people.

Leaders should understand, intellectually if not viscerally, the thousands of slights that most people, especially those who are poor, powerless, and different, encounter throughout their lives. These incidents, in the aggregate, rob people of their dignity and convey disrespect to them. It's not by accident that the verb "diss," to describe an active form of disrespect (as in "He dissed me"), originated among minority kids in inner cities. And it's not only the poor. My wife's experiences have sensitized me to the occasional "invisibility" in social settings of being a woman of small stature. An accomplished African-American professional colleague urged me to watch the difficulty she encountered in trying to get airtime at a meeting to make a point and make it stick in a mainly male work group.

These slights may be part of the fabric of daily life if you are short, or a woman, or part of an underrepresented race or religion. But that makes it all the more important for leaders (meaning you) to be conscious of and fight against your own unexamined, and even deeply buried, assumptions (prejudices) based on these qualities. The only factor that should matter is excellence and the potential for excellence.

The flip side of this kind of disrespect is love. (No, not that kind of love. I have nothing to add to that subject and would only confirm that leaders must not engage in it with those they lead.) I believe that some leaders have the emotional capacity not only to treat people with dignity and respect, but to actually love the people they lead. This is true if by love we mean a deep emotional attachment, a strong commitment, and an intense desire to contribute to the well-being of those who are loved. When it happens, it's a rare, wonderful, and complicated thing. (Isn't love always?)

I speak from experience, having been on the receiving, observing, and giving ends of such situations. Irwin Miller loved Cummins Engine Company and its people, though I don't think that's a word he would have chosen to describe his sentiment. The same is true for the long-time leaders of two companies where I am a board member: Paul and John Gordon and their family business, Gordon Food Service, and Terence Adderley of Kelly Services, a company founded by his father, William Russell Kelly. Again, "love" would not be their language. For my part, I'm happy to say without qualification that I loved the University of Michigan Business School and our people, hundreds of faculty and staff, thousands of students, and tens of thousands of alumni during the decade I was dean. And many, many of them reciprocated, which created a magical experience for me as a leader.

Are there risks and problems in leaders loving their organizations and people? Of course. I remember a director of a company that was undertaking major layoffs commenting on the matter of fairness in deciding who would be laid off first: "Remember, you always eat last the chickens that you've named!" I remember hearing a legendary investor say that it's unfortunate that companies have names. He thought it would be better if they just had numbers, so investors wouldn't become emotionally attached to them! Nevertheless, though there is a risk of becoming too deeply attached, I firmly believe it is a risk worth taking.

See and Develop the Potential in People

When leaders look at their people, what do they see? Some see what economists call "factors of production." Some see a lump of cost: salaries, benefits, and overhead expenses. Some see personnel problems, all that pesky griping, too many sick days, potential grievances and lawsuits.

But the best Mammalian leaders see one glowing, overarching thing when they look at people. They see *potential*. Potential to achieve the organization's mission and goals, then create new ones and achieve them, too. Potential to solve every problem the leader is concerned about and new ones that will inevitably appear. Potential to create, innovate, and grow the organization into something of enduring value.

I don't want to romanticize this notion excessively, but neither do I want to back away from my strong assertion that Mammalian excellence means believing deeply in people and their potential. Even the most humanistic and developmental leaders know that people are "all of the above." Yes, they are piles of problems as well as bundles of potential. What characterizes Mammalian excellence is that the view of people as reservoirs of potential trumps all the other equally real, more problematic human guises. And excellent Mammalian leaders *act accordingly,* making the learning, growth, development, and full contributions of their people their main business, rather than primarily focusing and acting on the risks of "being had" by the relatively small number of liars, cheats, and slackers in their employ.

I want to testify that I have been repeatedly amazed at what Mammalian leaders can unleash by spotting talented people and inviting and challenging them to do something new and difficult or take on more responsibility. When the leader accompanies this with expressions of belief in the person's ability to master the challenge, offers guidance at critical moments, and reinforces progress as it is made, wonderful things can and do happen. Here is an example.

When I was appointed interim president of the University of Michigan, I went right away to meet the president's secretary, Erika Hrabec. As soon as we started to talk, I knew from her accent that she was from the north of England, like my daughter-in-law, who is from Liverpool. Erika seemed to be a little shy and self-effacing, conscious of "her place." She was "just" a secretary, albeit the president's secretary. But I also suspected that, as with many self-made people, she was smart; not in an Oxford-educated, "posh" way, but in a street-smart, knows-people-and-how-to-get-things-done way. In addition, I had heard that she was hard-working, dedicated, reliable, and loyal, and that she was underchallenged relative to her native ability, her ambition, and her desire to contribute and grow.

To make a long story short, I told Erika that she was my assistant, not my secretary. She and I were a team. She was vitally important to me and the president's office, and I would assume she could do anything I threw her way until she demonstrated she couldn't, which I didn't expect to happen often. I told her that my view of my job as president was that I represented the entire University of Michigan to the world and that similarly, she represented me to the world, and I wanted always to be proud of the way she represented us. I told her that she was in charge of my calendar and therefore of two of my most precious professional assets as a leader, access and time, and that I was entrusting her to manage both with extreme professionalism and thoughtfulness.

The Power of the Mammalian Approach: A Classic Study

A famous leadership study conducted in the 1930s investigated differences between "authoritarian," "democratic," and "laissez-faire" leadership by manipulating the way teachers behaved toward students.[2] Specifically, teachers took on a dictatorial, participative, or passive leadership style. The results? Under authoritarian conditions, students were more passive and demanded the leader's attention and approval. Under democratic settings, students showed less tension and hostility, and more cohesion and cooperation. Laissez-faire conditions promoted lower overall productivity, satisfaction, and cohesiveness.

Interestingly, productivity under authoritarian and democratic conditions was comparable, with one notable exception. When the authoritarian teacher left the room, what do you think happened? Everyone stopped working. Under democratic conditions, work continues even in the leader's absence.

My confidence in Erika was richly rewarded. She rose to every challenge and more. People told me after a few months that they couldn't believe she was the same person. Today, she serves Mary Sue Coleman, Michigan's current president, not only as her assistant but as the appointed leader of the president's office. To round out the story of the power of belief in people's potential, I'm happy to report that I invited Erika, an occasional jogger, to join me in a half-marathon and experience the satisfaction and joy of meeting a big challenge in an arena beyond work. As is her way, she expressed doubt about her ability to tackle this new challenge, then resolved to do it, then did it. We crossed the half-marathon finish line together. Well, not quite together; she put on a sprint at the end and beat me by a considerable distance!

Make It About Your People, Not About You

Being a leader can be a great ego trip: It's really fun to be somebody! But, paradoxically, being an *excellent* leader requires selflessness and an attitude of service. A related paradox is that strong leadership requires a substantial ego and rock-solid self-confidence, but also a well-contained ego and deep humility.

Robert Greenleaf captured these paradoxes well in his writings on servant-leadership. Greenleaf was a career manager at AT&T in its halcyon, monopolistic days. After retirement, from age 66 until his death in 1990 at age 86, he wrote, spoke, and taught extensively after writing a seminal essay entitled "The Servant as Leader." The Robert K. Greenleaf Center for Servant-Leadership highlights the core philosophy with Greenleaf's own words:

It begins with the natural feeling that one wants to
serve, to serve first. Then conscious choice brings
one to aspire to lead. . . . The difference manifests
itself in the care taken by the servant—first to make
sure that other people's highest priority needs are
being served.

The servant-leadership philosophy may come across
as quaint or simply a curiosity, especially after recent
years in which headlines have been dominated by
business, political, and nonprofit leaders whose philosophy might be summarized as "serve-me leadership." I am concerned that a generation of young
Americans has come to equate leadership with nothing
more than the opportunity to get power, get rich, get
whatever you want.

What other lesson can be drawn from abuses like
then–vice president Spiro Agnew taking cash bribes on
the steps of the Executive Office Building, and Richard
Nixon attempting to cover up Watergate, and the presidential "indiscretions" of the Clinton administration,
and the massive looting of the public company Tyco
International by its chairman, Dennis Kozlowski, and
the extreme self-dealing of leaders of American institutions like the United Way and the New York Stock Exchange? By my lights, each of these so-called leaders
and others of their ilk, including the American Catholic bishops who moved known child-abusing priests
from parish to parish instead of protecting their flocks
by confronting and coming down hard on these crimi-
nal clergy, were miserable failures as leaders. They neither served nor led. And they taught young people the
wrong lessons about what it means to be a leader.

Fortunately, there are leaders on the national and international stage who have set the right example. South African President Nelson Mandela and Archbishop Desmond Tutu seem to me to have served the people—all the people—of South Africa extraordinarily well through their leadership in the second half of the twentieth century. President Ronald Reagan was a man with ideas, the courage of his convictions, a desire to serve, and an aptitude for leadership. The outpouring of affection and respect at the time of his death in 2004 suggests that this was a man perceived by the majority of Americans as a servant-leader who did well for them.

More important, I think, than these iconic and distant figures are the legions of leaders we all encounter in our day-to-day lives, who are model servant-leaders. I think of people I have met, such as Wendy Kopp, the founder of Teach for America, and Steve Mariotti, the founder of the National Foundation for Teaching Entrepreneurship (NFTE). Wendy, whose story is well known, has mobilized thousands of young people to teach in underserved schools across the country. Steve founded NFTE while he was a public high school teacher in the South Bronx in New York City. He decided he had to do something that would bring hope and a constructive path to kids he saw going the wrong way. Since 1987, NFTE has taught "entrepreneurial literacy" to more than 60,000 low-income, underserved young people in the United States and around the world.

I think about all the plant managers, department heads, school principals, mayors, and other leaders at every level I have known—people who have simply led with passion, skill, and integrity; servant-leaders who have viewed leadership as a privilege, put their people's interests above their own, and contributed to making the world a better place. Wendy, Steve, and others like them are not saints, and they're not completely selfless; they'd be the first to tell you that. But in comparison with the dreadful role models at the highest levels who have dominated the news for so long, they're pretty darned admirable.

CAPABILITIES TO ACHIEVE MAMMALIAN EXCELLENCE

I believe that certain dimensions of strong Mammal leadership are personality-based and rooted in early childhood development. You can't turn a cold fish into a teddy bear. And yet there are things aspiring leaders should know and can work on that will make them far more effective on the people side of the leadership equation. The two most important are what I call the Dream Deal and the Leadership Triad. And there are others: being an effective communicator and listener, remembering that good ideas can come from anywhere, and maintaining a sense of irony and humor.

The Dream Deal

I think the greatest leadership recruiting story of all times is the way Steve Jobs persuaded John Sculley to give up his promising career at PepsiCo and become Apple Computer's CEO in the 1980s. PepsiCo was an established consumer products giant and Sculley was slated to become its chairman and CEO, a brass ring of major proportions in the corporate world. By contrast, Apple was a promising but struggling small company in the totally new industry of personal computing. Jobs recognized, as smart entrepreneurs do, that he needed professional leadership for his company. He spotted and sought out Sculley, who had a reputation as one of the best and brightest executives in the land. Sculley rebuffed Jobs's repeated advances and rejected the proposition that he leave Pepsi and join Jobs in running Apple.

Reportedly, Jobs finally made a sale with this brilliant line: "Look, John, do you want to spend the rest of your life selling sugar water or do you want to change the world?"

In one sentence he planted in Sculley's mind a powerful dream and offered him the opportunity to make the dream come true. That, in a nutshell, is the Dream Deal. When I teach students how to build great organizations and develop strong people, I tell them it's simple: just enable people to make their dreams come true by joining you and doing the organization's work with excellence. The thing I love about the Jobs/Sculley story is that it is a reminder that the best leaders don't just *accept* people's dreams as a given, they actually *plant new dreams* that trump the old ones. Then they allow the dreamer to fulfill those dreams by giving time and talent to the leader and the organization. That's the Dream Deal. For Sculley, his old piration of being chairman and CEO of Pepsi was supplanted with a new dream of changing the world through the power of information technology at the personal level as Apple's chairman and CEO. Now that's impressive, imaginative recruiting!

When you think about it, the Dream Deal—suggesting dreams and enabling people to make them come true—is the driver of the entire American free enterprise system from a motivational perspective. Would you like to own a home, send your kids to a good school, have a secure retirement, buy a beach house? With wealth, you can do all these things. How to achieve wealth? Start a business or get a job, save by earning more than you consume, and invest the surplus wisely. Do these things, and get a little lucky, and you can achieve your dreams. Achieved all your dreams? Not to worry. The American dream machine will give you plenty more to think about!

Of course, not every Dream Deal is about wealth and economics, as the Jobs/Sculley story illustrates. Many people want to make a difference in the world. They want to work with people they respect and admire; they want to be a member of an organization in which they take pride; or they have goals like world peace or a cleaner environment or universal health care that are larger than they can achieve by themselves. So they need to be part of an organization with a similar mission.

Smart leaders do two things exceptionally well in recruiting and motivating people. They understand eople's dreams and show them how joining up and performing at a high level will enable them to achieve those dreams. And they sell the organization's purpose and culture as a means of achieving dreams people either have or might want to consider adopting.

I did a lot of faculty recruiting as a dean. Early on, I gave every prospective faculty member a pitch about what a good school we were and what a great school we intended to become, and I always ended by saying wouldn't it be exciting to be part of that adventure. What I learned is that this pitch went over very well with some candidates and like a lead balloon with others. I discovered that there were some really good candidates who had a singular dream—for example, to become the world's leading expert on insider trading, or to create a center on sustainable development, or to develop the next generation of faculty by being a mentor to doctoral students. These were the things about which the people cared passionately, and they were pretty much all they cared about. They would join whatever institution offered them the best chance and the strongest support to fulfill their very personal dreams. With faculty candidates like these, I learned to stifle the "we're going to be great and you'll love being part of it" pitch and, instead, focused like a laser on how much we cared about insider trading or sustainable development or doctoral education. I made sure the candidates knew we would do a better job than anybody else in enabling them to make their personal dreams come true.

Perhaps this all sounds good. But there are, inevitably, complications. For example, how can we know what people's dreams are? An experience with my little grandson, Bernie, reminded me that it's not always easy. Here's what happened.

When Bernie attended nursery school, auditions were held for the annual Christmas pageant. (I guess you even have to try out for things in nursery school nowadays!) Bernie got the part of Joseph. Since Joseph was the husband of Mary and one of the three members of the Holy Family, we all thought this was a pretty good part for a very young actor.

My son, Brian, told us that shortly after Bernie got the part of Joseph, he seemed downcast. When the two of them were driving home together from school one day, Brian asked Bernie if anything was wrong. He sought to reassure him by saying that he and Bernie's mother were pretty excited about Bernie playing Joseph. There was silence for a couple of minutes. Then Bernie looked down and said quietly, *"Dad, I wanted to be the donkey."*

Who would have guessed it? But I've found over the years in leading adults at work that there are many surprises about people's aspirations and dreams. I'll never forget being in the MBA program at the Harvard Business School when the dean announced that a distinguished senior faculty member was leaving the school to enter the degree program in Harvard's College of Architecture. I was amazed. At the time, I was considering starting a doctoral program in order to try to achieve, over many years, what he was about to leave! I couldn't imagine someone giving up what for me seemed a nearly impossible dream. But that's the nature of dreams: They form, and if we're lucky we achieve them, and then they give way to new dreams and possibilities.

I've learned to listen, observe, and even inquire directly in order to discover what the dreams are of the people who look to me for leadership. Whenever I could find a match between what someone wanted and what I could create that would serve the organization well, I did so.

I once heard Steve Jobs say that the best companies don't just ask their customers what their needs are and then fulfill them. Rather, they understand their customers so well that they identify their needs and wants better than they can and then fulfill them. Think about it. No customer ever asked for the Macintosh computer or the iPod, two enormously successful and much-beloved products.

There is a parallel in the Dream Deal. An insightful leader can sometimes envision a talented person doing something challenging and important when she has never even thought of it. Remember Jobs and Sculley. Or picture Sandy Weill shocking then-thirty-seven-year-old financial analyst Sallie Krawcheck with a completely unexpected invitation to head Citicorp's Smith Barney. You can imagine then, that offering a Dream Deal is one of the most pleasurable aspects of being a leader. And the results can, at times, be amazing!

As the story of Bernie and the donkey illustrated, it can be tough to know what people's individual dreams are. But fortunately, at a collective level, people's dreams are quite predictable. The best politicians know this and have a great ability to articulate our dreams in a way that leads people to say, "That person really understands."

For the leader who masters the Dream Deal, everything is possible when it comes to recruiting and motivating talented people.

The Leadership Triad: Stretch, Support, Connect

An organizational development group reported to me at Cummins Engine Company. One of our assignments from the president was to figure out why some of our managers were more effective at "making change" than others and why some had a superior track record of developing managers under them. We observed, studied, documented, thought, discussed, argued, and arrived at the following conclusion. The managers who led change most effectively and those who developed leaders most successfully shared a common approach that we were able to synthesize and describe simply as "stretch-support-connect."

> *Stretch* means creating a challenging picture of the future to which you want your organization to aspire, sometimes out of necessity (e.g., in the face of new competition or cost pressures), sometimes as a matter of choice (e.g., mission shift or striving to go from good to great).

> *Support* means two things. First, understand people's hopes, dreams, fears, and anxieties in the face of change; articulate them on everyone's behalf; and address them as fully as possible.

Second, ensure that people have the resources they need, such as authority, direction, expertise, and your support and confidence, to do their part in the change process.

Connect means putting the right people in touch with each other, ensuring that the right conversations and coordination are occurring, and providing everyone with the milestones of progress to keep them on the same page and moving forward.

At Cummins, I saw stretch-support-connect leadership in change management as we took 30 percent out of our costs and revamped our entire engine product line in record time. We called this initiative the Thirty-Month Sprint and reported monthly to the entire organization on our progress in product development, cost reduction, and other vital measures. Managing change does, indeed, involve plans, budgets, and project management tools. But the human side of change must be tended, also, and what people need from their leaders is a big stretch vision, a great deal of support, and a lot of connecting to each other, to resources, and to measures of progress.

I had stretch-support-connect in mind during every one of the 4,000 days that I led the University of Michigan Business School. It helped us achieve the changes I had in mind: a far richer education and development experience for our students, an endowment that grew from $30 million to $270 million, improvement in our national rankings, and accolades as the most innovative, top business school in the world. The Leadership Triad really helps produce organizational change.

It also produces individual change and development. Let me explain.

"Stretch" in individual development means envisioning an improved you, then setting goals and challenging yourself to meet them. What do you want to be? Perhaps you'd like to become a great teacher instead of a good one, fit and healthy instead of a couch potato, or a great leader instead of an ordinary one. Odds are that you can do it. In American life, there aren't just second acts but also third acts, fourth acts, and more!

In my experience, the role of a leader when it comes to the stretch dimension of development is to plant possibilities in people's minds. "Have you ever thought about sharpening your public speaking skills?" "You know, it probably hasn't occurred to you and you may not even be interested, but I think you could be an awfully good department chair." "I know you don't think of yourself as athletic—I never did— but there's this run-walk method that allows even people like us to complete a half-marathon successfully; shall we try it together?" I have said each of these things (and many more) to people with whom I worked over the years, and it's been amazing to see a little seed of an idea grow into achievement and development.

"Support" in individual development means providing people with what they need, when they need it, so they can keep on going. Here's an example: When I was a senior in college, a stretch goal I set for myself was to go to the Harvard Business School and earn an

MBA. I read an article about HBS in *The New York Times* Sunday magazine during senior year when I was a little adrift about my future. The portrayal of the school as an energetic, engaged institution with talented people that for decades had been a gateway of opportunity to leadership and success made a big impression on me. I applied and was accepted.

There were several things I didn't know during the happy months between acceptance and arrival in Boston. I didn't realize that the HBS class was 800 students, not eighty (I guess I didn't do my homework very well) and that, as a result, it was a big, impersonal place in which you, as a student, sometimes felt like a part going through a metal-stamping plant. I didn't realize that there would be an environment of intense individual competition among students fueled by plenty of faculty intimidation and overload. And I didn't realize that at age 22, I would be among the very youngest, least mature students in our class, mixed in with military officers who had served in the Vietnam War, CPAs, and other classmates with a lot of experience already under their belts.

During September, the first month of classes, all this hit me hard. I decided that I had made a serious mistake, didn't belong there, and was either going to flee or fail. I called my parents in distress and told them I was quitting the program.

My dad's reaction was that he could understand my decision. He suggested that I come home on Friday after classes and relax with him, my mother, and my fiancée. When I arrived home with my tail between my legs, what I got was a welcome with no scrutiny or interrogation about my problems at HBS. On Saturday, I started to talk about it. My dad made it clear that the decision was completely up to me. By Sunday, we had begun to discuss options and I asked him what he thought would be best. "You know, you've paid your tuition and room and board for the semester. Why don't you go back, attend class, and see how things go?" This seemed sensible, so I did as he suggested. Twenty-one months later I graduated from the Harvard Business School with honors. I'll be forever grateful to my father for providing me with just the right support at a time of crisis.

I think that I deeply internalized my parents' wise way of offering me support in this and other crises. When I was dean at Michigan, I often described my office as "a pit stop on the fast track" for our students, faculty, and staff. People knew they could come to me at any time, close the door, and discuss their frustrations, fears, disappointments, and occasional failures. My job was to listen carefully then metaphorically change their tires, fill their tanks, clean their windshields, give them a cool drink, offer a suggestion or two on race strategy or driving technique, and get them back on the track. Occasionally, I had to tell someone that the racing career was over. But most of the time, the leader's job in providing support is to offer a brief respite, encouragement, a bit of perspective and advice, and then get people moving forward again.

"Connect" in individual development means ensuring that people have the means and resources to develop. For example, surveys show that many people fear public speaking as something to be avoided at all cost. Jerry Seinfeld once joked that "according to most studies, people's number-one fear is public speaking. Number two is death. Death is number two! Now, this means to the average person, if you have to go to a funeral, you're better off in the casket than doing the eulogy." Yet effective public speaking is vital to many roles in life, both professional and personal (like toasting at weddings and eulogizing at funerals). I have connected many people over the years to Toastmasters, a wonderful organization dedicated to getting people up on their feet and speaking with increased competence and confidence.

In short, the triad of stretch-support-connect can be an enormously helpful guide to a leader striving to change an organization successfully or help people grow and develop. It's a great diagnostic tool: "What does this organization or person need at this moment that I can provide to enable continued progress?" And it's a terrific reminder that most of the time, helping organizations and people move forward is a positive process. There is, undeniably, the occasional need for a stern talking-to (I've given many such lectures) or a swift kick (support comes in many forms!). But what most organizations and most people need most of the time are new challenges to embrace, perspective, breathing room, someone to believe in them, and resources and tools to meet the challenges they've decided to take on. In other words, they need *stretch-support-connect* from their leaders.

Be an Effective Communicator and a Good Listener

This is especially true in our era of instant communications when people expect timely, unfiltered communications between them and their leaders. Nothing builds trust more than talking straight to people.

Leadership scholar Howard Gardner argues that leaders achieve effectiveness chiefly through the stories they relate and the vision they convey. They tell stories about themselves and their groups, about where they are coming from and where they are headed, about what it means to be feared, struggled against, and dreamed about. It is important that leaders be good storytellers, but equally crucial that they embody that story in their lives.

There is a time for broadcasting when you're a leader. But much more of your time should be spent asking questions, listening, observing, and learning. Irwin Miller told me something very valuable: "Leaders need to worry a lot more about what they *don't know* is going on than about the problems of which they're aware." How do you learn what's going on? Be curious, ask, observe, and listen, listen, listen.

Remember That Good Ideas Can Come from Anywhere and Anybody

This is a good antidote to the hierarchical nature of organizations and the assumption that more good ideas reside at the top of the pyramid than in the middle and bottom. In my experience, it just isn't true. Where good ideas reside is in creative people who are closest to the work. Good leaders make sure people at every level know their ideas are welcome, respected, and valued; that there are ways and means for them to participate and contribute; and that whenever possible, people's good ideas for improvement will be enacted.

Maintain a Sense of Humor and Irony

Our time on earth is short and, as Jimmy Buffet sings, some of it is magic and some of it is tragic. Leaders have an obligation to bring a sense of perspective to their people, especially in pressurized situations. Irony and humor can help immensely in this regard. Here is an example. I mentioned earlier my late friend Mike Walsh, with whom I worked at Cummins. Mike died tragically of brain cancer at age 53. He was an extraordinary leadership talent whose life was extinguished far too early. He had a great sense of humor. One day Mike broke us up with a funny line about the importance of rationales in management.

There are a lot of things you have to do in management just because you have to, and you need a palatable rationale to offer for public consumption. Talking someone into "voluntarily" resigning is a good example. When the time comes to communicate the person's departure, the announcement doesn't say, "Joe Blow is leaving the company after twenty years of extraordinary service because we decided he wasn't cutting it any longer and told him that he better resign before he got fired." Instead, it says, "We are grateful to Joe Blow for his long service and dedication to the company and understand and accept his decision to devote more time to his family and personal interests."

A group of us was crafting a rationale for a business decision one day during an especially stressful period at Cummins when Mike, stealing a line from the movie *The Big Chill* said, "Hey, did you ever think about what's more important, rationales or sex?" We looked at him in a daze; this was a group, after all, that was putting in fifteen-hour days, six days a week. "No, really, did you ever think about that?" he continued. "It's obvious that rationales are more important. When was the last time you went a whole week without a rationale?"

A Case Study in Mammalian Leadership

Here is a story that illustrates the sort of high-pressure, high-stakes people challenges that senior leaders face from time to time and how Mammalian leadership can win the day.

When I was appointed interim president of the University of Michigan in January 2002, succeeding Lee Bollinger, who became Columbia University's president, I inherited responsibility for the university's decision to defend the practice of affirmative action in our undergraduate and law school admissions processes. The university had been sued by two white applicants with the assistance of the Center for Individual Rights in Washington, D.C. The cases had made their way through the court system with various rulings, and the Supreme Court of the United States had announced its decision to hear and rule on the cases.

At issue now: *Who would defend the University of Michigan in the affirmative action cases before the U.S. Supreme Court?*

The university had been defended in the lower court cases by an outstanding attorney, John Payton, an African-American with a distinguished record in civil rights litigation who was a partner in the prestigious Washington law firm of Wilmer Cutler

Pickering. Payton's assumption was that he, and he alone, would represent us and argue our cases before the Supreme Court. (Understand that arguing, and especially winning, a Supreme Court case of historic importance and great social consequence is a pinnacle professional experience for a great attorney. Understand also that great attorneys have egos that match their reputations and their hourly rates.)

What I discovered when I became interim president was that President Bollinger had approached a different attorney, Maureen Mahoney, a partner in the Washington law firm of Latham and Watkins, to help represent the university in the affirmative action cases before the Supreme Court. Mahoney is a white, Republican woman, and at the time of her engagement she had an impressive win/loss record in cases she had argued before the Supreme Court. It became clear to me in conversation that Mahoney thought that she, and she alone, would be representing the university in the affirmative action cases. I also discovered that John Payton had no inkling of Maureen's involvement. I remember thinking to myself that my situation was just like the one described in the opening of the old *Mission: Impossible* TV show:

> President White, your assignment, should you choose to accept it, is to inform each attorney that there is another attorney who expects to represent the University of Michigan in these historic cases before the Supreme Court. You are to decide whether one of these attorneys will ultimately represent the university then dismiss the other without causing undue hard feelings and a possible public spectacle. Or you may decide that they should work together to defend the university, in which case your job will be to persuade two individuals of opposite political persuasions

and large conflicting egos, both of whom are angry at you, the client, to do so. Good luck. This tape will self-destruct in sixty seconds.

A number of senior people with whom I conferred on this difficult matter urged me to bite the bullet and choose one attorney, some favoring one, some favoring the other. I spent time with both attorneys, sized them up personally, and listened to threats to bolt if I tried to put them in a harness together. But gradually I came to the conclusion that if only I could do exactly that—persuade them to work together constructively and bring their respective strengths and perspectives to the arguments before the Court—then the university would have the very best possible representation. I viewed this as vital, since the value of affirmative action in admissions to our highly selective institution and our freedom to make admissions decisions were at stake.

Ultimately, my colleagues and I persuaded Maureen and John to work together. They represented us jointly and well before the Supreme Court. John took the lead in the undergraduate case, Maureen in the law school case. In a close vote, the university prevailed, affirmative action in admissions was upheld as a compelling national interest (with some important corrections dictated by the court in precisely how we take race into account in admissions decisions), and we retained authority over and freedom in our admissions decisions. Justice Sandra Day O'Connor declared a hope, which I share, that affirmative action, while still necessary, would be made obsolete and unnecessary by social progress over the next quarter century. Both John Payton and Maureen Mahoney did an excellent job in representing the University of Michigan, and they worked effectively as a team.

How did I help achieve "mission impossible"? By being a

good Mammalian leader. I never accepted the advice or the threat that if we urged John and Maureen to work together, one of them would walk. I knew that we were in a position to enable both of them to "make their dreams comes true." It would not be inconceivable, but it would certainly be unlikely for big-league attorneys to give up the opportunity to argue historic cases before the Supreme Court of the United States unless they felt "dissed" by the client. So I treated both attorneys with great respect and I offered them a rationale that enabled them to say "yes" to sharing the cases. The rationale was simply that my singular goal as president was to have a configuration of legal representation that would maximize the university's probability of prevailing in these highly consequential cases. I told Maureen and John that I was confident the two of them, with their distinguished records, their complementary points of view, and their respective specializations in the cases, represented the ideal configuration.

I am happy to report that this approach worked. Mammalian excellence was required and it proved successful.

In Chapter 6 we turn to the greatest challenge of all in your professional development: building on your Reptilian and Mammalian capabilities and adding more to become a Great Leader.

**Great
Leader
Requirements**
Innovative
Risk Taking
Appetite for Talent
Helicopter View
Sparkle Factor

**Reptilian
Requirements**
"Cold-Blooded"
Disciplined
Economic Sense
Financial Management
Verify, Control
Follow Up
Attention to Detail
Cool, Detached
Analytical

**Mammalian
Requirements**
"Warm-Blooded"
Nurturing
People Sense
Communications Ability
Trust, Delegate
Empower
Attention to Context
Warm, Engaged
Developmental

Foundation Requirements
Desire to be in Charge
Ability, Strength, Character

The Secret of Becoming
a Great Leader

I told you the secret of *being* a Great Leader in Chapter 1. Let me repeat it here.

To be a Great Leader, you have to be successful at *achieving change*—important, consequential change in the results for which you are responsible. Making change successfully is a leader's greatest challenge.

In this chapter, I want to share with you the secret of *becoming* a Great Leader. The secret is that there are five qualities Great Leaders share and that you can, to a degree, develop within yourself.

As shown on the top of the Leadership Pyramid, they are:

- Being innovative

- Being an intelligent risk taker

- Having an appetite for top talent

- Developing the "helicopter view"

- Exhibiting the "sparkle factor"

In this chapter, I will illustrate these qualities by focusing on Abraham Lincoln, perhaps America's greatest presidential leader, as well as a variety of modern-day leaders.

ABRAHAM LINCOLN AND THE LEADERSHIP PYRAMID

When I moved to Illinois in January 2005 to assume my responsibilities as president of the University of Illinois, I resolved to learn all I could about Abraham Lincoln. Illinois is, after all, the Land of Lincoln.

At the 2005 grand opening of the fabulous new Abraham Lincoln Presidential Library and Museum in Springfield, Illinois, my wife and I attended a "state dinner," modeled after one from the 1860s, and were transported back 150 years. My new hometown of Urbana was part of the circuit Lincoln rode during his years as a central Illinois attorney. And I am proud to have as a colleague Phillip Paludan, a distinguished professor at the University of Illinois at Springfield and one of the nation's great Lincoln scholars (*The Presi-*

dency of Abraham Lincoln, University of Kansas Press, 1994).

Abraham Lincoln is an ideal introduction to Great Leaders. He was a great leader, of course, arguably the best in America's presidential history, and certainly the right person for the times. I think you'll find it interesting to learn more about Lincoln through the lens of the Leadership Pyramid. Most of what made Lincoln a great leader applies to those of us in all kinds of leadership roles who are striving to achieve excellence.

Lincoln had the foundation requirements for leadership: a driving (though concealed with modesty) desire to be in charge and extraordinary ability, strength, and character. He was a flawed man, afflicted by depression, moodiness, and occasional serious errors in judgment (for example, his early appointments of generals who let him down badly in the prosecution of the Civil War). But his core values, superior intelligence, ability to communicate, mental and physical toughness, and personal resilience fully qualified him to become a leader.

Lincoln was a man who felt deeply (great empathy can be a consequence of the curse of depression). This quality enabled him to exhibit Mammalian excellence as a leader. Lincoln was deeply affected by the deaths of his mother, a young love (Ann Rutledge), and his young sons. Perhaps as a result, he was an exceptionally sensitive man. He often paid attention to the advice of others (he grew a beard, for example, when Grace Bedell, an eleven-year-old girl in Westfield, N.Y., suggested it in a letter). As a child, he had an aversion to cruelty and bloodshed and was known for scolding other children for senselessly hurting animals (". . . an ant's life was to it as sweet as ours").

Lincoln prized rational thinking and an analytical approach to problems, an essential requirement for Reptilian excellence as a leader. This is reflected in many of his speeches. Americans know Lincoln best for the Gettysburg Address ("Four score and seven years ago . . ."), which was composed of fewer than 300 words, about one typed, double-spaced page by today's standards. In fact, though, most of Lincoln's great orations, as in the Lincoln-Douglas debates of 1858 and his Cooper Union address in 1860, were lengthy, reasoned analyses of the nation's situation and what to do as tensions grew between anti- and pro-slavery forces. Indeed, Lincoln feared uncontrolled emotion. In one address, he stated that "passion . . . will in future be our enemy" and that the nation must rely on "reason, cold, calculating, unimpassioned" reason to determine its direction in turbulent times.

Lincoln was also capable of acting with toughness when necessary, another requirement for Reptilian excellence. This was best demonstrated in his determined prosecution of a bloody war despite his personal aversion to cruelty and bloodshed. Lincoln's toughness showed itself in other ways, too. For example, in 1863–1864, during exceptionally dark days for the Union war effort, Lincoln threatened to jail and exile judges who used the writ of *habeas corpus* (which requires those detaining a person to show proof and justification for the detention to a judge) to interfere with the draft, and then, in an action that reverberates with controversy to this day, he simply suspended the writ throughout the country.

But these qualities alone did not make Abraham Lincoln a Great Leader. Foundation requirements and Reptilian and Mammalian excellence by themselves never make a leader great. It is the ability to make change, consequential change in the areas of results for which the leader is responsible. And Lincoln delivered.

LINCOLN AND THE FIVE QUALITIES OF GREAT LEADERS

What made Lincoln a Great Leader is that *he achieved great results* (he subdued the Confederate rebellion, thus saving the Union) and *he envisioned and produced truly consequential change* (he ended slavery, giving millions of Americans their freedom). How did Lincoln do it? The same way other Great Leaders produce results and make change:

- They are innovative and don't succumb to conventional wisdom.

- They take calculated but significant risks that pay off.

- They surround themselves with extraordinarily talented people and bring out the best in them.

- They have an unusual sense of perspective, looking ahead, back, and sideways.

- They have personal qualities—presence, charisma, magnetism—that make them "sparkle."

At the risk of oversimplifying, let me illustrate these five qualities of Great Leaders by applying them to Abraham Lincoln.

Innovation: Great Leaders Are Original Thinkers

Lincoln was quick to see that the "policy difference" over slavery was life-threatening to the very concept of the United States. He famously, and economically, conveyed this belief with a Gospel reference that spoke to the Bible-reading, religious people of Illinois in his acceptance of the Republican nomination for senator from Illinois in 1858 (a race he lost): "A house divided against itself cannot stand."

Lincoln's true innovation as a leader was to eliminate slavery. But the process of innovation is usually messy. For example, despite his clarity of thought, Lincoln did not, let us admit, set out to become the Great Emancipator. His journey to the Emancipation Proclamation was difficult, at times tortured, flexible, and creative. While Southerners thought him the devil incarnate because of his opposition to the spread of slavery, Lincoln was despised by others because he sought, time and again, creative compromise rather than declaring himself an unwavering abolitionist.

In a completely different vein, Lincoln, like all Great Leaders, exhibited tremendous curiosity about new things that might enable him to achieve his goals—

in Lincoln's case, winning a war. For example, he spent many hours with a man who claimed he could save thousands of lives and millions of dollars by providing better predictions of the weather (he couldn't). Similarly, he took a personal interest in new weapons proposed by inventors, on occasion trying them out on the back lawn of the White House.

Risk Taking: Great Leaders Are Informed Risk Takers with a Track Record (but Never a Perfect Record) of Success

Although Lincoln was maligned by his detractors for being too cautious, he evidenced a greater willingness to "roll the dice" than many of those on whom he counted for leadership in his administration.

Nowhere was this more evident than in his strategic and tactical differences with his generals in the first several years of the Civil War. Generals McDowell, Halleck, and McClellan all let Lincoln down, in many instances by a lack of aggressiveness and unwillingness to press an advantage, once created. Lincoln faced a problem familiar to all leaders: how to get subordinates on the same page, in terms of risk taking, without undermining their authority, autonomy, and sense of responsibility. Time and again he tolerated his generals' excessive conservatism, dropping broad hints, even issuing orders . . . but to little avail. For example, General George McClellan appeared to have what it takes—he was a brilliant organizer and a great strategic planner—but his timidity, hesitation, and risk aversion frustrated Lincoln. As many a leader has found, it is only after changing out inferior leaders for stronger ones that the desired results get accomplished. In Lincoln's case, the decision to replace McClellan with Ulysses S. Grant and William Sherman helped the Union prevail in the war.

The pattern of Lincoln's decisions—to engage in war to save the Union, to issue the Emancipation Proclamation, to tip in the direction of forgiveness and reconstruction rather than punishment and isolation of the Confederate states—reveals an impressive level of thoughtful risk taking, guided by clear goals and high moral purpose.

Spotting Talent: Great Leaders Have an Insatiable Appetite for Outstanding Talent

These leaders know innately that the only way to overcome their own limitations of time and ability is to surround themselves with the strongest people. Unlike lesser leaders, they are not threatened by talented people. Rather, they seek them out, understand their goals and dreams, and enlist them in pursuit of their shared aspirations.

Lincoln was extraordinary in this respect. Indeed, the title of historian Doris Kearns Goodwin's book, *Team of Rivals* (Simon & Schuster, 2005), says it all. Lincoln populated his cabinet with some of the ablest leaders of his time, including two who were bitterly disappointed that it was he, not they, who won the Republican presidential nomination and ultimately the presidency. William Seward, Lincoln's secretary of state, and Salmon Chase, his secretary of the treasury, both believed themselves far better qualified than Lincoln to lead the country. But he reached out after his election victory and persuaded each to join his administration and serve the country.

Helicopter View: Great Leaders Have an Extraordinary Sense of Perspective

As a private citizen, candidate for office, and elected official, Abraham Lincoln kept his feet on the ground, but he also rose above immediate conflicts and controversies to look ahead, behind, and around and offer people vitally important context and perspective.

Today we call this the helicopter view.

It is not by accident that Lincoln began the Gettysburg Address by looking back eighty-seven years to the founding of America ("our fathers brought forth, upon this continent, a new nation") and ended minutes later by looking ahead hopefully to the time when "this nation shall have a new birth of freedom, and that government of the people, by the people, and for the people shall not perish from the earth." This was the helicopter view brought to a solemn occasion, as President Lincoln reminded all present, in broad historical terms, of the *context and purpose* of the sacrifice of those laid to rest at the battlefield.

The Sparkle Factor: Great Leaders Have Presence

Some light up a room by virtue of their personality and appearance. Some are the life of the party. Some have a *gravitas* such that they may say little, but whatever they say has great impact. Some have magnetism and charisma. Although it is impossible to sort out how much presence flows from the role and its authority and power, and how much flows from the individual, there is, in great leaders, a quality I call the "sparkle factor."

Lincoln's persona in the minds of most people is serious and melancholy. It would probably surprise you to know that long before he was "anyone" in the sense of being a public figure, Lincoln was frequently the life of the party. A great storyteller, he also enjoyed pranks, like the time in Springfield that he wrote shrewdly funny newspaper columns under the pseudonym "Rebecca" to attack Democratic policies and make fun of an office holder.

Observed by many to be an extraordinarily homely man, it was Lincoln's intelligence, wit, command of language, morality, and humanity that produced a sparkle that helped him win leadership positions and earn the respect and affection of millions.

GREAT LEADERS TODAY

What is the relevance of Abraham Lincoln as a Great Leader to leaders of the modern era . . . and to you?

Just this: Today, as throughout human history, the very best leaders are those who produce great results and bring about consequential change. They may do so on a small scale, turning around a school or manufacturing plant—or even just a work group—that is in trouble, or floundering, or underperforming relative to its potential. Or they may do so on a large scale: Nelson Mandela and Archbishop Desmond Tutu led a thirty-year campaign while imprisoned and out of power, respectively, to end apartheid and bring majority rule to South Africa.

Often the job of a leader is (to quote a recent best-seller) to transform an organization from "good to great."

We find Great Leaders in every arena. Jack Welch was an extraordinary value-creating CEO at General Electric. Steve Jobs created one industry with the invention of the Macintosh and transformed another with the invention of the iPod. Dr. Martin Luther King, Jr. brought an end to official discrimination while bringing greater dignity and respect to the lives of millions of Americans. Herb Kelleher transformed the U.S. airline industry over a thirty-year period by quietly building an airline—Southwest—on a different business model, achieving consistent profitability, and forcing the rest of the industry to move in his direction.

As change makers, Great Leaders are, first and foremost, *innovators.* They are original thinkers and often contrarians. They are usually guided by a few powerful ideas. Henry Ford originated the idea of the assembly line and the $5 day. Ronald Reagan: Freedom is good, communism is evil. Abraham Lincoln: Union good, slavery bad. Tom Monaghan, founder of Domino's Pizza: Simple menu, good product, we'll bring it to you.

For Sam Zell, arguably the founder of the modern real estate investment trust (REIT) industry, the big idea is "liquid real estate." Warren Buffett challenges the conventional investment wisdom to avoid putting all your eggs in one basket by diversifying. What's wrong, he asks, with putting your eggs in a single basket and watching that basket very closely, as he does in Berkshire Hathaway?

Doris Christopher, a University of Illinois graduate in home economics, and her husband Jay founded The Pampered Chef in 1980 with a few thousand dollars. Doris's idea was that good kitchen products would help homemakers create good meals that would bring families together and strengthen family bonds. Twenty-five years later, the company was acquired by Berkshire Hathaway, the ultimate compliment for an American entrepreneur.

Change makers today and forever must be *risk takers.* Nothing changes without a leader placing bets that might, and sometimes do, fail. The chairman of a company was asked why he hired as his successor a fellow who once led a business venture that failed and cost the company $50 million. "Because," he said, "a fellow has to fail once in a while in order to learn how to take intelligent risks. He's already paid his tuition in that school."

Most successful leaders will acknowledge that luck—pure chance—played a role in their success. Surely the mounting economic problems of the former Soviet Union played as big a role in the collapse of communism as Ronald Reagan's challenge, "Mr. Gorbachev, tear down this wall!" Deregulation of the airline industry in 1978 contributed to the success of Southwest Airlines and Herb Kelleher, who founded the airline in 1971. Luck plays a role in the success of

Great Leaders because they must take risks—roll the dice—and although risk can be limited in a variety of ways, it cannot be removed from the equation.

The best leaders realize that because their aspirations are great, they can't do it all themselves. Thus, they develop an insatiable *appetite for talented people.* They know they need people different from themselves and better than they are in order to achieve those aspirations. (One of the little secrets in higher education is that conventional A students often end up working for creative and entrepreneurial C students.)

Great Leaders are not necessarily the easiest people to get along with because they are responsible for results and therefore expect excellence. The best of them not only expect but encourage and enable others to excel. Their appetite for talented people is also reflected in their tremendous curiosity about the world and the ideas that drive the world. They ask a lot of questions, and if you have ideas, they're likely to milk you dry!

Great Leaders understand the power of ideas. They may or may not be book smart, but they are curious about how the world works and how that relates to their goal or dream.

Years ago, I learned that many executive search professionals ("headhunters") look for two things as they size up people for senior leadership jobs. Most people have never even heard of these qualities, yet candidates for top jobs are routinely screened in and out of searches based on them!

One is the "helicopter view." Most of us would describe this as a sense of perspective. Can the person put an immediate problem, question, or challenge into a larger context of the past, the future, things going on concurrently in other spheres, and perhaps most important, the larger mission and purpose to which it relates? And can the person do it not just as an intellectual exercise but, rather, identify the practical consequences of context?

Let's say, for example, that you are the new CEO of General Electric, the world's greatest large-growth company. You are succeeding Jack Welch, who for twenty years was one of the greatest value-creating CEOs in history. As you consider the company's strategy and its current businesses, you pause to look ahead. What you see coming is a tsunami of spending on health care because of an aging population and a biological revolution. You also note that "sustainability," a concept that was marginal just a decade ago, is rapidly becoming mainstream as concerns about environmental degradation grow. Finally, you reflect on the philosophy of your predecessor, who worked intensively on reengineering the company and improving quality processes. You decide that this has been good, but that improvements have perhaps come at the expense of innovation and creativity.

As a result of all this thinking—a helicopter view of GE and the world—you decide to place major new strategic bets. You acquire some medically oriented companies, combine them with your medical systems division, and create a new business called GE Healthcare. You decide to be a major factor in environmental businesses and combine this strategy with a commitment to innovation that you label "eco-imagination." And so on.

These are exactly the strategic bets that have been made by Jeff Immelt, Jack Welch's successor. They are the product of a helicopter view of the company and the world.

The other quality is the "sparkle factor." Every Great Leader has a special something that creates an unusual *presence*. That presence flows not only from the role, but from the individual. It's personal and it's compelling.

Sparkle comes in different forms. Brilliance. Charisma. Moral depth. Being well spoken. Striking appearance. Intensity. Energy. Great Leaders come with a wide variety of personalities, from extroverted to introverted, from intense to relaxed, from intellectual to interpersonal. There is no formula for "sparkle." But you know it when you see it.

For example, I've had the opportunity several times in the last year to meet Barack Obama, the junior U.S. senator from Illinois. Senator Obama has an abundance of the sparkle factor. He is intelligent, well spoken, interpersonally warm, energetic, and thoughtful. He exudes and articulates moral depth. He has overcome adversity to become a high achiever. If I were handicapping the political future, I would bet on Senator Obama being America's first African-American president. Why? Because he has it all, and "all" is best summed up as "sparkle."

LEADING FOR INNOVATION

The first requirement to become a Great Leader is to be innovative yourself and to foster innovation in your organization. The reason is that most organizations and institutions fail or underperform because they do not (or cannot) adapt to changing times, technologies, culture, standards, and expectations. Therefore creative thinking by a leader, and the ability to recognize the valuable creative thoughts of others, is the foundation of being a Great Leader.

But thoughts are not enough. Great Leaders must enable their organizations to convert new ideas into action and results to produce consequential change. This is tough to accomplish but vital for success. Let me explain.

In many ways, the ultimate yin and yang of leadership is to figure out how to simultaneously exercise effective *control* (a dimension of Reptilian excellence), which requires organization, order, and discipline, while also ensuring large-scale and widespread *innovation,* which requires creativity and, frequently, a degree of disorder and irreverence.

This we can say with confidence: No organization ever achieved long-term prosperity through control alone. Although good control is *necessary* for survival, innovation is vital for prosperity. Great organizations hungrily seek out more effective ways to do things at every level. They are highly adaptive. They reinvent themselves regularly. These capabilities, essential to successful adaptation, share one common requirement: an inclination, appetite, and ability to innovate.

What can I tell you about leadership for innovation? A lot.

I was thrilled when, in the late 1990s, the University of Michigan Business School was named the nation's most innovative business school by *Business Week* magazine in its semiannual rankings issue. I was thrilled because when I became dean in 1991, I remember thinking we might never be the richest business school, or the oldest, or the snootiest. But we could be the most innovative, the one most willing to come up with and adopt intelligent new ways of educating and developing our students so they would knock the socks off the companies that came to us as a source of talent.

What I learned about leading to encourage innovation is played out every day in the world's most creative companies like Apple Computer, Pixar Animation Studios, 3M, Honda, and others. Leaders who want their organizations to be innovative need to do four things: Expect it; energize it; start and shape it; and nurture and protect it.

Perhaps you're disappointed that there's not more magic in this list. But the fact is that innovation is like every other good thing that leaders want their organizations to achieve—growth, efficiency, good people development, and so on. It always starts with expectations.

Early on, success is fragile and later people get worn out, so the leader needs to energize the effort. Leading by example is always impressive, so having an innovative idea yourself now and then is helpful. More important, though, is recognizing the innovative ideas of others, then throwing your weight behind them with recognition, resources, and praise. Finally, innovative ideas are fragile, so they need to be nurtured with support that only the leader can provide. The organizational mainstream will often try, through outright hostility or benign neglect, to squelch innovations (they're a nuisance) and the people who come up with them (they're often a nuisance, too). So the leader must protect both.

How Does an Organization Become Innovative?
Organizational research has yielded a number of key findings:[1]

- A leader's favorable attitude toward change leads to a climate conducive to innovation.

- Participatory work environments facilitate innovation by increasing employees' awareness, commitment, and involvement.

- Successful adoption of innovation depends largely on the leadership, support, and coordination that managers provide. Managerial support is especially critical during the implementation stage since this is when coordination and conflict resolution are essential between individuals and units.

"Presumption of Yes." As dean of the University of Michigan Business School, I gave careful thought early on to how to create a climate of high expectations with regard to fresh ideas that would lead to innovation and change. I came up with a simple philosophy that I communicated to everyone in leadership positions at the school. I simply called it the "Presumption of Yes."

I realized that every day, students, faculty, staff, alumni, and friends of the school experienced things that they thought we could do better. And they were right. For example, students hated waiting in line to buy their course materials. Faculty members teaching classes wanted to know that every classroom would be clean and ready for their use with a standard audio-visual setup and teaching supplies. Companies that hired our students wanted them ready to hit the ground running with excellent analytical, problem solving, and communications skills, as well as knowledge of economics, marketing, and so on. Many of our students wanted to have international experiences in various parts of the world while they were in the program to prepare themselves for the global world of business. And so on.

Those of us who ran the school did our best to anticipate and solve these problems. But I noticed that often we were on the defensive, When people complained, we tended to say, in one form or another, things like, "You don't understand," or "We can't afford it," or "We already tried that." Often these responses were accurate and true. But not always, and worse, the effect of our unreceptive attitude was to discourage any further offering of ideas by members of our community. We inadvertently shut down a vital wellspring of ideas for innovation. People kept doing things the same old way except when *they* decided to change them. Meanwhile, we squandered a lot of goodwill among people who wanted to love their school and make it a better organization.

How could we break this idea logjam, open the floodgates, and move to a much higher level of innovation across the school? My answer was a leadership philosophy: the Presumption of Yes.

At a Monday morning meeting of the school's Quality Council—made up of about twenty-five of the school's leaders—I announced that henceforth, when anybody in the community came to one of us with an idea for improvement, there would be a "Presumption of Yes"—yes, we're going to do that! (I was inspired in this regard by my executive assistant at the time, Sheryl Smith, whose response to every idea, problem, and possibility that came her way was a cheerful, "We can handle that!" followed by action and results.)

I told the Quality Council that for every good idea that came forth, there would be only two possible outcomes: implementation or a timely, considered, and persuasive reason why we wouldn't do it, including feedback to the initiator of the idea. I told the council members that if complaints about ideas they had rejected came to me, I would support their decisions, but only if *I* was persuaded by them. Otherwise, I would reverse them and direct implementation of the rejected idea.

The results of the "Presumption of Yes" were amazing. For nearly a decade, new things large and small occurred at the school at a prodigious rate. Members of the community felt empowered. And the leaders of the school at every level came to see that many ideas that would have been rejected out of hand in fact had merit and could, with creativity and effort, be implemented. After a while, innovation simply became a way of life at the school, and many new things happened as a result. For example:

- Some of our students, especially African-Americans, wanted to be able to spend time on business projects in various African countries. We created the African Business Development Corps (and it was while visiting this program one summer that I met Archbishop Desmond Tutu).

- Another group of students who believed in the team-building and personal empowerment effects of outdoor adventure experiences created an M-Trek orientation program with a little support from the school.

- Faculty members who were exploring a new intellectual area and wanted to share their emerging knowledge with students in the classroom were stymied by the fourteen-week, forty-two-hour course requirement; in response, we created seven-week, twenty-one-hour courses, reducing the barrier to entry of timely new knowledge into the curriculum and expanding the number of elective offerings.

- Students who wanted more job opportunities on Wall Street and in Silicon Valley suggested we make it easy for companies to hire them by going to the companies instead of making them come to our Midwest campus. As a result, for years I led Wall Street and Silicon Valley recruiting trips, accompanied by hundreds of students. The companies were delighted.

Some of the new things that people wanted *didn't* happen. But there was always a good reason. Here's an example.

For years there had been a wrangle between our library staff and a small number of students (night owls,

I assume) who felt that the library should be open all night, every night. Library staff resisted, citing reasons including cost and security. The students would argue, "Stay open and they will come." Library staff would respond, "No." It got a little ugly.

Following the "Presumption of Yes" philosophy, I told the library staff that I wasn't convinced by their argument. We needed to move from the realm of conflicting opinions and high emotion to fact-based decision making. I directed them to stay open all night for a month and to keep a careful record of library patronage, by the hour, from the old closing time (midnight) to the old opening time (8 A.M.). They did, and it turned out that the library staff was right. We never had more than a half-dozen patrons in the dead of night and we often had none. We showed the students the results and the cost of staying open. I won't say they liked the decision, but they understood and accepted it. The conflict went away.

Sometimes leaders have to take radical action to make things happen. The "Presumption of Yes" was radical, a calculated bet on my part, and a little scary at the time. But it really made things happen. I urge all leaders who want to kick up the pace of innovation in their organizations to adopt this philosophy.

SITUATIONS MATTER AND RESULTS COUNT

Great Leaders—the best of the best—are people who bring about consequential change. The last two words—*consequential* and *change*—deserve comment.

America's greatest presidents—George Washington, Abraham Lincoln, and Franklin Roosevelt—all served at times of profound crisis in the nation's history. Washington faced the challenge of birthing the country and serving in a position—president of the United States—that was literally without precedent. Lincoln faced the dissolution of the Union and enormous pressures on the institution of slavery. Roosevelt faced the devastating Great Depression of the 1930s and the Second World War. Indeed, all three presidents are closely associated in the minds of Americans with war—the Revolutionary War, the Civil War, and World War II.

Situations matter because great challenges create the opportunity for leaders to achieve great results and make consequential change.

It is also true that history is written by the victors. So for leaders, results count. Had the Berlin Wall not collapsed, had the former Soviet Union not imploded on his watch, Ronald Reagan most likely would have been viewed as he was at the midterm of his presidency—an amiable figure with conservative views who risked the health of the American economy to build American military might. But to what purpose? Without the wall and its collapse, it would not have been obvious. Success vindicates leaders. As John F. Kennedy said, "Victory has a thousand fathers but defeat is an orphan."

Perhaps it's hard for you to relate to the results on which presidents of the United States are judged. If so, here's a story you can relate to. It's about Craig Tiley, coach of the University of Illinois men's tennis team from 1993 to 2004, and the results he achieved.

As I've told you, Great Leaders can be found in every kind of organization. Craig Tiley was a Great Leader in University of Illinois athletics. He joined our staff in 1993 as interim coach of men's varsity tennis. When he was urged to toss his name in the hat for the permanent job, he did something different. He wrote out a one-page, ten-year plan to make the Illinois men's tennis team a national champion. His plan laid out a vision, values, a strategy, and benchmarks—three years out, six years out, and ten years out—and what needed to be accomplished in each time frame. Tiley got the job and then went about the hard work of turning his plan into action.

It paid off. Tiley led the tennis program from being a virtual unknown when the team went from four wins and twenty-three losses in 1992–1993, his year as interim coach, to the very top of college tennis ten years later, when the University of Illinois won the National Collegiate Athletic Association (NCAA) men's tennis title in its undefeated 2002–2003 season. Along the way, the team won eight consecutive Big Ten regular-season championships. Tiley groomed ten players to All-American status. In eleven years as head coach at Illinois, Tiley achieved a 249–73 record.

Accountability for achieving results is a hard reality that Great Leaders must embrace.

My boss at Cummins Engine Company, Jim Henderson, taught me a valuable lesson in this regard. Jim was a tough competitor determined to keep Cummins a winner in the diesel engine industry in the face of both severe domestic competition (Caterpillar and Detroit Diesel) and new foreign competition. In the early 1980s, when I was a member of the president's staff at Cummins, Jim did a masterful job leading a particularly important and difficult senior management meeting. We hammered out a plan to simultaneously keep our new product development plans on track and improve our operating performance while coping with a business downturn that was, for us, the most serious since the Great Depression.

"Great meeting!" I said to Jim as we walked out together. "Well, we'll see," he said. I was surprised by his subdued demeanor in the aftermath of what I viewed as a triumph, so I pressed him about what he meant. "Leadership is about results," he said. "What actually happens, what we achieve, whether we execute our plan, and whether our plan gets the job done are all that really count. And don't forget it."

I haven't.

We see every day that it is much easier for people to embrace the *privileges* of leadership than the *responsibilities*. Similarly, it is difficult for leaders to resist the temptation to make excuses, blame others, and even dissemble to avoid taking full responsibility for poor results. When the most senior leaders in organizations and society do this, it is corrosive because it teaches people at every level that an appropriate response to problem performance is to bob and weave instead of accepting responsibility.

So be a stand-up person: Take responsibility for results.

The final chapter is next. In it, I invite you to challenge yourself to become a Great Leader.

7

Challenge Yourself: Become a Great Leader

You have borne with me through many chapters and ideas. I've shared with you most of what I have learned about leadership.

Now I have to put the ball back in your court. There is only one person who can resolve to make you a leader or a better leader. That's you.

Though it sounds audacious, I urge you to challenge yourself to become a Great Leader. The reason is that we rarely achieve more than our highest aspiration and we sometimes fall short. To ensure you become a leader or a better leader, set your sights on becoming a

Great Leader. With hard work and some luck, you just might do it.

There is a paradox I want to point out to you. You can't become a Great Leader just by deciding that's your goal, any more than you can become a great musician or artist or golfer by deciding *that's* your goal.

So how do you do it? Well, to continue the golf analogy, you give yourself a chance to become a great golfer (and guarantee you will become a better golfer) by *developing your game*: driving, midrange, short game, putting, bunker shots, and so on. And by learning how to play well under different conditions: sunny days, rainy days, hilly courses, flat courses, courses with water, fast greens, slow greens, and so on.

The same is true of leadership. Once you aspire to become a Great Leader, you can forget about the goal. Instead, concentrate on *developing yourself* as a leader. Ensure you have the foundation requirements, work to achieve Reptilian and Mammalian excellence, and master the five additional qualities of Great Leaders, those people who can make change and achieve results. Use this book as your guide.

With that idea in mind, I have three parting thoughts for you:

- *Remember that developing yourself is a journey you can take but never finish.* I'll give you a few ideas about how to do it successfully.

- *Strive for good endings in your leadership work.* Leave on good terms and manage succession responsibly.

- *Be resilient.* How you cope with doubt, discouragement, disappointment, and occasional failure is vital to your success.

DEVELOP YOURSELF

As you know, to run the leadership race you have to put yourself on the leadership track. Opt at some time for a leadership role versus individual contributor work, then do your best and learn from the experience. Here's my story in that regard.

At the age of thirty-one, I had achieved tenure at the University of Michigan, where I was studying and teaching leadership and management. Achieving tenure was every young faculty member's goal. So, two years later, when I was invited to join the management of Cummins Engine Company, I gave up my university appointment with great reluctance. But it turned out to be the best professional decision I ever made. Going into the corporate world opened the door to twenty-five years of leadership practice, and it exposed me to many of the world's best leaders in the for-profit and nonprofit sectors. What I learned was this: When it comes to development, it's very important that early career achievements and a desire for security not become a gilded cage that thwarts your growth. Even if you choose to stay in a job or an organization for a long time, you must be able to answer the question: How will I continue to stretch, grow, be challenged, and put myself in close proximity to people from whom I can learn?

Is Your Job Developmental?

Enhance your leadership abilities with five key challenges identified by research.[1]

1. *Job transitions* involving changes in scope, function, employer, content, or location require finding new ways of thinking about and responding to problems and opportunities (i.e., moving from a line to a staff position).

2. *Creating change* requires action and strategic decisions in the face of uncertainty (i.e., starting a business from scratch or turning around a business in trouble).

3. Jobs with *higher levels of responsibility* have greater breadth, visibility, and complexity. The stakes are also higher and may require more interfacing with key external players.

4. *Influencing people* not under your direct authority, such as peers, clients, or cross-functional task forces, teaches leaders how to build relationships, handle conflict, and be straightforward.

5. Dealing with *obstacles* or difficult situations, such as a problematic boss or an unsupportive group of top managers, can develop success strategies as well as increase perseverance and self-confidence.

Now that you've put yourself on the leadership track, the next step is to use the Leadership Pyramid to evaluate your strengths and weaknesses and develop yourself as a leader.

The Leadership Pyramid offers an ideal framework for understanding how leaders develop. Three central concepts should guide your thinking about leadership development:

- *Natural Bias.* In my experience, every person enters the leadership development journey with either a primarily Reptilian or primarily Mammalian bias. The bias is rooted in personality, talents, parental guidance, education, and early work experience. For example, Abraham Lincoln, whom we discussed in Chapter 6, probably came in on the Reptilian side of the pyramid, drawing on his experience as a lawyer and his belief in a rational, analytical approach to problems.

- *Vertical Development.* Whether one's natural bias is Reptilian or Mammalian, vertical development means building natural strengths, abilities, and inclinations to a higher level of competence. For example, a good accountant becomes a CPA, then a strong controller, and ultimately a respected chief financial officer. This job progression exemplifies a Reptile's vertical developmental journey as each experience builds directly and naturally upon the preceding one.

- *Spiral Development.* "Spiral development" means taking on experiences, assignments, and

challenges that strengthen your weak or less
natural side at ever-higher levels of
responsibility. This is what athletes call
"learning to play to your weak side."
Mammalian leaders have Reptilian experiences
in order to develop a more Reptilian mind-set
and skill set, and vice versa.

For example, my natural bias was Mammalian. I
started out as an organizational behavior professor
(read Mammal), then became a corporate human resource executive (Mammal again, with a first dose of
Reptile), then a business school dean (combining Reptile and Mammal and developing some Great Leader
abilities). After that, I became interim head of an asset
management firm (a very Reptilian industry). Along
the way I did a major study of internal control and
headed the audit committee of the nation's largest
apartment real estate investment trust (Reptilian development). Now, as president of a great university, I find
myself drawing deeply every day on all dimensions of
leadership and doing my very best to achieve excellent
results and make positive and consequential change.
Only time will tell, of course, if I will be successful.

Figure 7-1 is a graphic representation of these concepts of natural bias and vertical and spiral development, using the Leadership Pyramid.

Here's a good story about the spiral version of leadership development. It involves David Neithercut, whom
you met briefly in Chapter 3. I introduced him there
as a great young Reptilian leader, the extraordinarily
talented chief financial officer of Equity Residential

Figure 7-1. The Leadership Pyramid as a framework for leadership development.

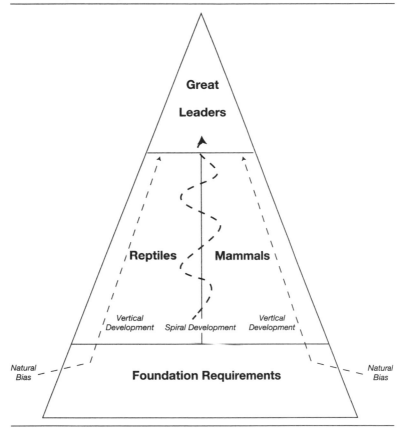

(NYSE: EQR), the nation's largest apartment REIT. Just recently, Dave was appointed chief executive officer of the company, a testimony to his growth over the years. This is the story of one small piece of that growth.

In the mid-1990s, several of us on EQR's board of trustees heard rumblings of concern from Dave's colleagues at Equity Residential despite, or perhaps because of, his brilliance. The concerns were what I think of as "the usual suspects" in senior management difficulties: inadequate listening, poor communication (in this case, assuming everyone gets things as quickly as you do), and a touch of arrogance.

Another trustee and I were impressed by Dave's raw talent and Reptilian strengths, so we quietly intervened. I like to think that we helped make a small contribution to Dave's development as a leader. We urged him to go for a week to the Center for Creative Leadership (CCL) and get some guidance on improving his leadership abilities, based on "360-degree feedback" from the people with whom he worked.

A few days after Dave got back from CCL, I received a package in the mail. I opened it and found a length of two-by-four with a bronze plaque reading, "Thanks, I Needed That! Dave Neithercut."

Recipe for Success

Tests of high-achieving, motivated individuals suggest that they spontaneously and consistently engage in goal setting, envision successful performance, assume responsibility for accomplishing their goals, anticipate obstacles and ways to overcome them, are highly persistent, take calculated risks, and use feedback (their own and that of others) to measure performance.[2]

He was right. There are times when most of us would benefit from a two-by-four across the nose from someone who cares about us and our development. Today, having invested for many years in his leadership skills, the trustees of Equity Residential have made a bet that David has the makings of a Great

Leader and have named him CEO—a happy story of leadership development.

Here's one other suggestion to help you develop yourself as a leader. It is to understand not just your *job* (e.g., as manager of purchasing or vice president for manufacturing or dean) but your *roles*. Jobs describe your *responsibilities*; roles describe your duties and what you actually *do*. Thus, they are a tip-off to the skills you need to do your job well.

Let me give you a personal example. When I became dean of the University of Michigan Business School, I decided that I had five roles:

- Chief academic officer

- Chief personnel officer for the faculty

- Chief budget officer

- Chief fund-raiser

- Chief spokesman and salesman for the school

I analyzed my preparation, readiness, and skill level for each of these roles on a 1 (poor) to 5 (excellent) scale. I gave myself a 5 as chief personnel officer and three 4s in other key roles, but only a 1 as chief fund-raiser. I had had almost no experience working with donors to raise money. This really alarmed me!

So, on the day after my appointment was announced, I called a wonderful man, the late David Hermelin, who was a graduate of the school and a great fund-raiser, and asked him to be my teacher. He agreed. We met for a couple of hours each month for a year, and the rest is history. I became a happy and accomplished fund-raiser with David's guidance.

Identify the roles of your job and evaluate yourself on each, so that you can develop yourself aggressively where you find yourself wanting.

STRIVE FOR GOOD ENDINGS

Every leader's run comes to an end. Sometimes it is carefully planned and managed. Sometimes it is sudden and unexpected. Endings and succession go hand-in-hand. Ideally, senior leadership in successful organizations is a well-run relay race over many decades. The baton is passed smoothly from one leader who has run his leg of the race successfully to the next runner who does the same. A few organizations do this well; GE comes to mind. All too often, however, it doesn't work out that way.

I remember the Old Testament story of Judith's battle with Holofernes, the leader of the Assyrians. When Judith cut off Holofernes's head and displayed it to the Assyrian army, they behaved as if they had all lost their own heads and were then easily routed by the Israelites. If the Assyrians had less of a leadership cult and greater understanding of the chain of command, perhaps the outcome would have been different. Analogous situations can be observed after the departure of a charismatic leader in present-day institutions. Those left in the organization are often in disarray and may even withhold followership from the person appointed as a replacement, disabling this person from leading.

I urge leaders to remember that effective succession is a vital, and final, measure of their performance. Researchers examining executive succession effects in 193 companies across a nineteen-year time span found that leadership accounted for nearly half of the variance in profit margins and stock prices.[3] Thus it is good for board members and senior executives to remember that effective succession—deciding who will have the privilege and responsibility to run the next leg of the leadership relay race—is their single most important responsibility.

Perhaps the most common obstacle to good endings and orderly succession is the tendency of many leaders to hang on to their jobs for too long. I decided when I became dean of the University of Michigan Business School that ten years would be about the right length of time to serve. So, I resolved to serve for a decade and not be dissuaded from my plan.

My logic was that the average tenure of deans was about five years, and most of them seemed to me not to accomplish nearly enough in that period of time. But I had also seen deans who stayed for fifteen and more years whose departure was greeted with a big sigh of relief from all concerned. So while there is no science to the matter, I liked the idea of leading long enough to make a big difference—get in, learn the ropes, set goals, assemble a team, and work long and hard to achieve strong results—but not staying so long as to get stale or wear out my welcome. Ten years seemed to me about right and that's exactly what I did.

My point is not that ten years is the right length of time for every senior leader to serve. Rather, it is valuable to see a leadership job not as a sinecure or a sentence of indeterminate length, but as a period of one's life in which to serve with great passion, energy, and enthusiasm, then give it up and move on to do something else. All kinds of good things flow from this approach:

- It creates a sense of urgency in the leader to accomplish a lot, because time to do so is limited.

- It enables the leader to pace herself since the length of the run is known.

- It makes clear to the governance group responsible for succession that they have a job to do and when they'll need to do it.

- It keeps potential successors interested and working hard because they know they won't have to wait forever to have their shot and get their futures resolved.

- It requires and enables the leader to plan for life after the present assignment. Leaders often hang on simply because they don't know what to do next.

So I urge every leader to create a presumptive plan for intended length of service, convey it to others, and stick with the plan unless there is a compelling reason not to. (P.S: Changing your mind because you decide you don't want to give up the job is not a compelling reason. It's not by accident that there is a term limit for U.S. presidents!)

When the dust settles in every succession drama, there is one winner and many losers. Or, to state it differently, there is one person who is flush with the thrill of success and several people who are coping with feelings of failure and disappointment.

Five Hardship Lessons

Researchers have identified five typical hardships leaders face and the lessons they teach.[4]

Hardship	Lessons Learned
Career setbacks	Self-awareness
	Organizational politics
	What one really wants to do
Personal trauma	Sensitivity to others
	Coping with events beyond one's control
	Perseverance
	Recognition of limits
Business mistakes and failures	Handling relationships
	Humility
	How to handle mistakes
Problem employees	How to stand firm
	Confrontational skills
Downsizing	Coping skills
	Recognition of what's important
	Organizational politics

I don't need to say a lot about handling success; it's one of life's most pleasant experiences. I've rarely felt better than in the days and weeks after being appointed an officer of Cummins Engine Company, dean of the University of Michigan Business School, or president of the University of Illinois. Of course, it helps to be gracious in triumph and remember that your success is not the centerpiece of other people's lives (indeed, it can be a little irritating). The short honeymoon period after getting a big leadership job is full of confirmation, congratulations, and optimism. The problems can wait!

But what about failure to get the nod and dealing with the inevitable disappointment? That's where resilience comes in.

BE RESILIENT

You know by now that I am an Abraham Lincoln buff. Every leader should read and remember Lincoln's story. It reminds us that even the most brilliant leaders, including Lincoln, who saved the Union and ended slavery, suffer periods of doubt, discouragement, disappointment, and failure. How you endure and overcome them may well make the difference between your success and failure as a leader.

It is remarkable to realize that in the run-up to the presidential election of 1864, only months before the successful end of the Civil War, Lincoln was convinced that he would not be reelected for a second term. He openly discussed preparations for the handover of the Office of the President to his successor. He was extremely discouraged about his electoral prospects. Many in his administration shared his pessimism.

Lincoln won reelection decisively.

Was Lincoln simply an inveterate pessimist, steeling himself for the possibility of disappointment? Perhaps. But every senior leader knows the lonely moments when you wonder whether anyone understands what you are trying to accomplish; whether your detractors and doubters might be right in their relentless criticisms of your intentions, plans, and actions; and whether it will ever all come good. If you're a leader and you haven't had these moments, I might wonder if you're prone to nonstop mania.

In Chapter 3, I discussed the meaning and importance of being a high-integrity leader. Here, I want to remind you of the importance of being a *resilient* leader. For my money, integrity and resilience are the two most important dimensions of a leader's character.

Resilience means that in the face of adversity, you keep going. It means that although you don't ignore your doubts, you have the courage and confidence to either maintain your course or change it only after rational analysis and careful decision making. It means that when you experience a failure, you admit it, reflect on it, and learn from it. It means that when you are disappointed, you experience it and understand it, then face the future and move ahead.

Let me give you another personal example.

When I served as interim president of the University of Michigan in 2002, I wanted the permanent appointment to the presidency in the worst way. I loved the university and had proven my ability as a leader while serving as dean. Everyone acknowledged that I was doing an admirable job as interim president, and for better or worse, I fell in love with the job and the people with whom I worked.

I remember noting to a close colleague at the time: "Well, I've now proven I can *do* the job; but can I *get* the job?" The answer, ultimately, was no. The regents of the university selected Dr. Mary Sue Coleman, who was then president of the University of Iowa, to be Michigan's next president. Dr. Coleman, for whom I have the highest regard, became the first woman to serve as president of the University of Michigan in its 185-year history.

That decision created a very tough moment in my professional life. While my head accepted the decision, my heart didn't. I found myself quite alone in figuring out how to cope with my intense feelings of disappointment, anger, and embarrassment at not having gotten the nod.

I decided to take on the experience of severe disappointment directly; that is, to fully engage it, think about it, and talk and write about it rather than deny, rationalize, or dodge it. What follows are excerpts from the remarks I made to the regents and officers of the university at a dinner organized to thank my wife, Mary, and me for our service during the interim presidency. This sort of event can be an awkward, even a dreadful, experience for all involved. But it doesn't have to be.

On Disappointment
Remarks to Regents and Executive Officers
B. Joseph White
July 18, 2002

It is kind of you to recognize and thank Mary and me for our service to the university through the interim presidency.

I want to say a serious word this evening about a topic seldom discussed in our success-oriented society, and that is the experience of disappointment.

It's no secret to anyone in this room that I'm disappointed not to be able to serve the university as president in the years ahead. Now, just before you think, "Oh, my gosh, I can't believe he's talking about this," let me assure you that my message about disappointment is a fundamentally positive one. I would say that, above all, disappointment, serious disappointment, is a clarifying experience if one chooses to fully engage the emotion and think about it constructively, rather than try to deny or rationalize it.

There is, first, the issue of how to respond. Realizing that I would need to vacate the president's office in the Fleming Building, I found myself thinking back to the famous 1944 newspaper picture of an angry and disappointed Sewell Avery, the chairman of Montgomery Ward, being carried out of his office by the National Guard after losing an argument with the federal government over a wartime emergency measure and refusing to leave office. This seemed to me not the way to go!

The most crucial matter is how to think about a disappointment when it occurs. There is little choice over how to feel about it: Shock, sorrow, anger, and sometimes embarrassment are, to a degree, inevitable. But perhaps there is an opportunity for choice in thinking about the matter.

In this regard, my good friend David Gray sent me a quotation from a commencement speech he heard by Stephen Covey, the "Seven Habits" guru, at Marquette University:

> *"I remember being in the stacks of a library . . . and pulling down a book which had three sentences in it which so staggered me, they profoundly influenced the rest of my life. These were the three sentences: Between stimulus and response is a space. In that space lies the freedom and our power to choose our response. In those choices lie our growth and our happiness.*
>
> *"In other words, between all that has ever happened to us and our response to it, is our power to choose our response. We are not fundamentally a product of nature or nurture, we are fundamentally a product of our choices to both nature and nurture, and we can decide deep within ourselves what represents true north, what represents the deepest orientation of our life, and if we do that, inspired with a God-centered lens, we will find our true identity and our mission."*

Now, I'm not sure that this theory of choice would pass muster with the university's cognitive psychologists and neuroscientists. But it presents a concept of human choice and free will that I embrace. We can choose how to think about and react to disappointment. At the extremes, one line of thought leads to bitterness and a shriveled soul; the other leads to wisdom and growth.

Framed properly, career disappointment, to cite one example, can help clarify in other ways. For example:

- What is really important in our lives? For me, the enormous value of the love of a spouse and children, and the support of friends, has never been clearer. Indeed, Mary and I have received more expressions of affection and respect than one virtually ever gets . . . without dying first! The love of our children has been extraordinary. My son, for example, decided that I now need a new challenge. The result is that I will be joining him in a half-marathon in London on September 29. I'm well into the training for it, with great physical and mental health benefits.

- Who, in fact, am I, with one professional identity removed and a new one not yet formed? What will be my work, my contributions, my sources of satisfaction and self-esteem? How will I define success? In this regard, I have been inspired by the words of Emerson on what it means to succeed:

"To laugh often and love much; to win the respect of intelligent persons and the affection of children; to earn the approbation of honest citizens and endure the betrayal of false friends; to appreciate beauty; to find the best in others; to give of one's self; to leave the world a bit better, whether by a healthy child, a garden patch, or a redeemed social condition; to have played and laughed with enthusiasm and sung with exultation; to know even one life has breathed easier because you have lived . . . this is to have succeeded."

Disappointment is a deeply humanizing and empathy-building experience. Few human beings live a life as abundant and blessed as we who have lived in the second half of the twentieth century in the United States of America, with good educations and good jobs. No matter what our troubles or disappointments, we are surely among the most fortunate people who have ever lived. The truth is that the disappointments that are rare for us are routine in the lives of many of our fellow citizens, not to mention the billions around the world in truly difficult and unfortunate circumstances. It has become a joke in our society to use the term "I feel your pain." It shouldn't be.

Let me conclude simply by saying that I wish for none of you the pain of disappointment. But we all know that disappointments have occurred and will occur in our lives. What I do wish for you is full engagement of the emotion, careful thought about your reaction, a successful fight against the bitterness that can flow, destructively, from disappointment, and a rapid and successful recovery.

Mary and I thank you, again, for the opportunity to serve our university.

When I began these remarks and the guests realized that I was actually going to talk about *it*—that is, about not being appointed president—you could hear a pin drop. It was pretty tense. But at the end, to my surprise, there was spontaneous applause and a long, standing ovation.

Word of these remarks somehow made their way to Joann Lublin, a columnist for *The Wall Street Journal*. In April 2003, in her career column, she featured the subject of dealing with disappointment and cited my experience and remarks. It was a little daunting to have over two million copies of a well-read newspaper feature my one big career disappointment. But I agreed to the story for this reason: I decided that if my success in coping with disappointment could help even a few people avoid the bitterness and loss of confidence that often flow from disappointment, it would be worth it.

In fact, I received many letters after the column ran, including a memorable one from a man who said he had been deeply embittered for twenty years because of a career setback and resolved after reading the column to put it behind him and get on a positive, constructive path. I hope he succeeded.

I share my remarks with you because I discovered in this experience that how you handle the inevitable disappointments in a long professional career says a lot about who you are and what your future prospects are likely to be. Disappointment handled well builds and demonstrates character, increases respect for you, and makes you wiser and more resilient. Disappointment handled poorly will diminish or even destroy you.

Although we often think we know what we want in life, the truth is more complicated. It's impossible to know what really will be best for us. And when we work hard to overcome adversity, great things can happen.

Buddhism on Disappointment

"The master held up a glass and said, 'Someone gave me this glass, and I really like this glass. It holds my water admirably and it glistens in the sunlight. I touch it and it rings! One day the wind may blow it off the shelf, or my elbow may knock it from the table. I know *this glass is already broken,* so I enjoy it incredibly.'"

Achaan Chah Subato, Theravandan meditation master

I really wanted to be president of the University of Michigan. But not getting the job freed me to have a uniquely valuable professional experience on Wall Street, to live in Manhattan for a year (during which my wife and I devoured New York City like two kids in a candy store), to run three half-marathons, and to write this book. Am I glad not to have missed the chance to do all that! And now I have the extraordinary honor of leading another great institution, the University of Illinois. It's a wonderful new challenge.

Yes, I was lucky. But good luck following adversity is built on a foundation of facing it squarely and vowing to press on by always appreciating life's most important gifts.

Now you know why my message to you is: Be resilient!

FINAL THOUGHT

I've been asked over the years how to go about being a successful leader. In this book, I have given you a pretty complete answer.

My own journey of leadership development continues. Serving the University of Illinois with excellence is going to take all my abilities, natural and developed. And I know I can't do it by myself. It will require a great team effort.

What I know for sure is that I am going to give it my all.

I wish the same for you: a wonderful leadership challenge, great people with whom to work, and a personal commitment to learn, grow, and do your very best.

I hope you have found this book useful. More important, I hope it will help you become a Great Leader, achieve excellent results, and make positive and consequential change in your organization, whatever it might be.

Good luck! Our world needs you to succeed.

THE "NATURE OF YOUR LEADERSHIP" SURVEY

Research has demonstrated positive links between leaders' self-awareness and their performance.[1] Therefore, the following questionnaire is offered to give you insight into how you like to look at things and how you go about making decisions. As a current or aspiring leader, knowing your own preferences can help you identify your strengths, understand what kinds of work you naturally gravitate toward, and spot the next step of your leadership development quest.

Directions

Think of the times you have held leadership positions. They can be at work or in social settings (school, religious organization, etc). With these situations in mind, answer each question by writing a number in the blank space from 1 to 10. Remember, there are no right or wrong answers! (NOTE: For automated scoring, you can also take the survey online at www.thenatureofleadership.com.)

Strongly Disagree	*Neutral*	*Strongly Agree*
1	**5**	**10**

1. _____ I often emerge as a leader in groups.
2. _____ Perseverance is one of my strengths as a leader.
3. _____ People would describe me as a "considerate leader."
4. _____ I have a track record of leading consequential change.
5. _____ When leading I trust others with important decisions.
6. _____ I am a demanding leader.
7. _____ I have strong skills in finance.
8. _____ When making difficult decisions I detach myself from the problem.
9. _____ I am comfortable bringing ethical issues to the fore.
10. _____ As a leader I communicate a compelling vision.
11. _____ I lead with my heart.
12. _____ I am competitive by nature.
13. _____ People describe me as someone with remarkable "presence."
14. _____ A number of people at work consider me their mentor.
15. _____ I always carefully monitor those I lead.

16. _____ I have successfully led innovative changes at work.
17. _____ People would describe me as a "driven leader."
18. _____ I always utilize economic principles when leading.
19. _____ I am a strong public speaker.
20. _____ I often take on leadership positions.
21. _____ As a leader I've taken significant risks that have paid off.
22. _____ I always hold a position open till I find the right person.
23. _____ People connect easily to me.
24. _____ I have experience addressing ethical issues.
25. _____ I have very strong interpersonal communication skills.
26. _____ I always meet the ambitious goals I set.
27. _____ I have overcome serious adversity as a leader.
28. _____ People around me would describe me as an "original thinker."
29. _____ I always nurture the personal growth of those I lead.
30. _____ I have a strong desire to be in charge.
31. _____ I have competently analyzed financial statements.
32. _____ Discipline is one of my greatest strengths as a leader.
33 _____ I frequently involve people to make decisions.
34. _____ People would describe me as a "cold" or "distant" leader.
35. _____ I make sure everyone gets along at work.
36. _____ I command the respect of others.
37. _____ When faced with difficult choices I always make the rational decision.
38. _____ People describe me as "conscientious."
39. _____ I communicate a big picture perspective to my followers.
40. _____ As a leader I always get results.

Congratulations! The survey is complete.

CALCULATE YOUR SCORE

Calculate your scores on each dimension by adding up your numbered answers to the following questions:

Foundation Requirements Score			
Question Number:	Fill in Your Answers:	Sub-dimensions	Add Sub-dimensions
1.		Desire to Be in Charge	Desire to Be in Charge Total:
20.		Desire to Be in Charge	
30.		Desire to Be in Charge	
2.		Strength	Strength Total:
17.		Strength	
27.		Strength	
36.		Strength	
9.		Character	Character Total:
24.		Character	
38.		Character	
Total: (Add numbers)			

Mammalian Requirements Score	
Question Number:	Fill in Your Answers below:
3.	
5.	
11.	
14.	
19.	
23.	
25.	
29.	
33.	
35.	
Total Score:	

Reptilian Requirements Score	
Question Number:	Fill in Your Answers below:
6.	
7.	
8.	
12.	
15.	
18.	
31.	
32.	
34.	
37.	
Total Score:	

Great Leader Requirements Score	
Question Number:	Fill in Your Answers below:
4.	
10.	
13.	
16.	
21.	
22.	
26.	
28.	
39.	
40.	
Total Score:	

YOUR LEADERSHIP PROFILE

The framework utilized in this survey involves four leadership dimensions organized in a pyramid. The pyramid is fleshed out in more detail in *The Nature of Leadership* book, but get a taste of your natural leadership tendencies now!

Fill in your scores on the four Dimensions
(Possible points per category range from 10 to 100)

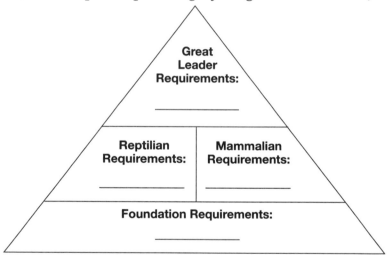

The Leadership Pyramid

WHAT DO YOUR SCORES MEAN?

Your Foundation Requirements

You can't be a great leader unless you have a strong desire to be in charge. This is not necessarily ego-driven. Usually it springs from a personal belief that you can guide, organize, and support others effectively to accomplish a goal—win a ball game, raise money, build a company, win an election. Your Foundation Requirements score measures this desire, as well as two other qualities that determine your probabilities of success as a leader: strength and character.

Your Desire to Be in
Charge Score: _____ (out of 30)

Your Strength Score: _____ (out of 40)

Your Character Score: _____ (out of 30)

Mammals vs. Reptiles

To build on your desire to lead, the leadership pyramid offers a Mammals and Reptiles metaphor. Briefly, Mammal leaders tend to be nurturing and warm, while Reptile leaders tend to be tough and calculating. Remember: leading involves balancing both a concern for people and a focus on getting the job done. Leaders must know how to be supportive, cooperative, and trusting, as well as tough, disciplined, and competitive. The key is knowing when to be what, and this poses quite a challenge for all leaders. What can help is knowing that you will naturally gravitate toward one or the other style.

Compare your Mammal and Reptile scores; the higher score clues you in to your preferred leadership style, or "natural bias" as a leader. Generally, higher scores are better, with two cautions. One, extreme disparity between Mammal and Reptile scores may be a sign that a leader is out of balance. Two, an extremely high score (e.g., 90 or more) may also indicate a problem (e.g., too calculating and controlling? too soft and sappy?). To get the most out of your survey scores reflect on whether the profile that emerges resonates with you, squares with the way others see you, and highlights for you the way you want to be as a leader.

Mammalian Leadership Preference

You lead with your heart and naturally gravitate toward people. You understand that people are what make an organization work and treating them fairly and humanely is key to getting the most out of people. Empowerment, mentorship, and communication are your strengths and they will serve you well in the leadership game. But relying too heavily on these skills alone can be a weakness and may undermine your efforts. In the book, pay particular attention to Chapter 4 on Reptilian Excellence—you can develop your opposite style to become a more complete leader.

Reptilian Leadership Preference

You lead with rational thinking, knowing that when it comes to leadership the head should rule the heart. You understand that strong, clear leadership—based on calculated decisions and economic principles—is required for your organization to survive in a competitive marketplace. This is your strength and it will serve you well in the leadership game. But relying too heavily on these skills alone can be a weakness and may undermine your efforts. In the book, pay particular attention to Chapter 5 on Mammalian Excellence—you can take advantage and learn about your opposite style to become a more complete leader.

Your Great Leader Requirements

Great leadership is about making consequential and successful change. The top of the Pyramid assumes that you have the ability to be hard and soft and the instincts and experience to know what each situation requires. Because great leaders are change makers, they are also innovators and intelligent risk takers. They have a boundless appetite to recruit and work with the most talented people. They possess a rare sense of perspective or "helicopter view." And they have a personal something special—presence, energy, charisma—known as the "sparkle factor."

Working on any of these dimensions will improve your Great Leadership Requirements score and your capacity for great leadership.

*   *   *

Now that you've done a self-assessment, you might want to have one or more people who know you well complete the survey *about* you. Then, compare their assessment of you with your self assessment. It will generate some interesting discussion!

We hope you enjoyed exploring the nature of your leadership and that the experience generated some developmental insights as you progress on your leadership journey.

N O T E S

CHAPTER 1

1. T. J. Bouchard, Jr., D. T. Lykken, M. McGue, N. L. Segal, and A. Tellegen, "Sources of Human Psychological Differences: The Minnesota Study of Twins Reared Apart," *Science* 250 (1990), pp. 223–228.

2. A. Howard, "Identifying, Assessing, and Selecting Senior Leaders," *The Nature of Organizational Leadership: Understanding the Imperatives Confronting Today's Leaders*, ed. Stephen J. Zaccaro and Richard J. Klimoski (San Francisco: Jossey-Bass, Inc., 2001), pp. 305–346.

3. M. W. McCall, Jr., and M. M. Lombardo, "Off the Track: Why and How Successful Executives Get Derailed," *Technical Report No. 21* (Greensboro, N.C.: Center for Creative Leadership, 1983).

4. Robert Hogan and Robert B. Kaiser, "What We Know About Leadership," *Review of General Psychology* 9, no. 2, (2005), pp.169–180.

CHAPTER 2

1. Robert R. Blake and Anne A. McCanse, *Leadership Dilemmas-Grid Solutions* (Houston: Gulf Pub. Co., 1991).

2. Patricia Sellers, "Hank Paulson's Secret Life," *Fortune Magazine* 149, no. 1, (January 12, 2004).

CHAPTER 3

1. J. M. Kouzes and B. Z. Posner, *The Leadership Challenge* (San Francisco: Jossey-Bass, 1995).

2. K. T. Dirks and D. L. Ferrin, "Trust in Leadership: Meta-analytic Findings and Implications for Research and Practice," *Journal of Applied Psychology* 87 (2002), pp. 611–628.

CHAPTER 4

1. For an interesting read on how success can breed complacency, see R. N. Foster and S. Kaplan, *Creative Destruction: Why Companies That Are Built to Last Underperform the Market—and How to Successfully Transform Them* (New York: Currency, 2001).

2. Steven McShane and Mary Ann Von Glinow, *Organizational Behavior,* 5th ed. (McGraw-Hill: New York, 2001), pp. 399–400. See also Solomon E. Asch, *Social Psychol-*

ogist (Englewood Cliffs, NJ: Prentice-Hall, 1952), Chapter 16.

CHAPTER 5

1. Cary Cherniss, *Beyond Burnout* (Routledge: New York, 1995).
2. K. Lewin, R. Lippitt, and R. K. White, "Patterns of Aggressive Behavior in Experimentally Created Social Climate," *Journal of Social Psychology* 10 (1939), pp. 271–279.

CHAPTER 6

1. Fariborz Damanpour, "Organizational Innovation: A Meta-Analysis of Effects of Determinants and Moderators," *Academy of Management Journal* 34, no. 3 (September 1991), pp. 550–590.

CHAPTER 7

1. Patricia J. Ohlott, "Job Assignments," *The Center for Creative Leadership Handbook of Leadership Development*, ed. C. D. McCauley, R. S. Moxley, and E. V. Velsor, (San Francisco: Jossey-Bass, Inc., 1998), Chapter 4, pp. 127–159.

2. Robert J. House and Ram N. Aditya, "The Social Scientific Study of Leadership: Quo Vadis?" *Journal of Management* 23, no. 3, (1997), pp. 409–473.

3. N. Weiner and T. A. Mahoney, "A Model of Corporate Performance as a Function of Environmental, Organizational, and Leadership Influences," *Academy of Management Journal* 10 (1981), pp. 453–470.

4. Russ S. Moxley, "Hardships," *The Center for Creative Leadership Handbook of Leadership Development,* ed. C. D. McCauley, R. S. Moxley, and E. V. Velsor, (San Francisco: Jossey-Bass, Inc., 1998), p. 197.

APPENDIX

1. A. H. Church, "Managerial Self-Awareness in High-Performing Individuals in Organizations," *Journal of Applied Psychology* 82 (1997), pp. 281–292.

INDEX

A C K N O W L E D G M E N T S

I have long believed in the value of partnership at work. I thank Yaron Prywes for partnering with me to create this book. I sought a smart, young person with an interest in leadership and found him in Yaron.

Deb Aronson was our editor and made valuable contributions to getting the book in shape for the publisher. I will always have fond memories of our work sessions in the solarium of the President's House in Urbana with Yaron on the phone from New York City. Thank you, Deb.

Adrienne Hickey of AMACOM Books chose to publish our work. There is no higher compliment to an author and his team. She brought a fresh eye to our manuscript and made deft suggestions that led to a much improved book. Thank you, Adrienne.

I am extremely honored that my colleague and friend, C. K. Prahalad, has written the foreword to this book. C. K. is one of the world's true original thinkers and a great teacher and adviser to leaders. His work on strategic intent, core competence, and serving the bottom of the pyramid has been groundbreaking and consequential. Thank you, C. K.

I owe a special thanks to all the inspiring leaders with whom I have worked over the years. Some but not all are featured in the book. People who played a special role in my development and understanding of leadership include:

- My father and mother, Bernie and Gena White, my grandmother, Mary Mezzetti, and my mother-in-law, Nancy Jean Vanderberg.

- Professor Harry Levinson of the Harvard Business School, who taught me that organizational life replicates family life and our first leadership models are our parents.

- Professors Paul McCracken, Dallas Jones, and Bill Hall, as well as Dean Gilbert R. Whitaker, Jr., and Wilbur K. Pierpont, all of the University of Michigan Business School.

- My leadership partners at the University of Michigan Business School in the 1990s, Paul Danos (now dean of the Tuck School at Dartmouth), Ted Snyder (now dean of the Graduate School of Business at the University of Chicago), Sue Ashford (the Michael and Susan Jandernoa Professor of Organization and Management at the University of Michigan), and Brent Chrite, now associate dean at the Eller College of Management, University of Arizona.

- J. Irwin Miller, Henry Schacht, Jim Henderson, and Ted Marston of Cummins Engine Company, as well as members of the Cummins' board of directors, including Hanna Gray, Don Perkins, Bill Ruckelshaus, and Frank Thomas.

- The leaders of companies on whose boards I serve, including Sam Zell of Equity Residential, Terry Adderley of Kelly Services, and the Gordons—Paul, John, Dan, Jim, and John, Jr.— as well as my colleague and friend David Gray, of Gordon Food Service.

- David Alger, chief executive officer of Fred Alger Management, Inc., a legendary investor of the 1990s and one of the thirty-five members of the Alger firm (including Ted Adderley, son of Terry Adderley) who died on September 11, 2001.

- Sheli Rosenberg and Jim Harper, fellow trustees at Equity Residential; Verne Istock and Maureen Fay, fellow directors at Kelly Services; and David Brandon, CEO of Domino's Pizza.

- Bill Davidson, chairman and CEO of Guardian Industries, the owner of the Detroit Pistons, and the benefactor of the William Davidson Institute.

- Mary Kay Haben, senior vice president of Kraft, and Alan Gilmour, retired vice chairman of Ford Motor Company, both of whom served as chairs of the University of Michigan Business School Visiting Committee.

- Great leaders of nonprofit organizations with whom I have worked, including Eleanor Josaitas and the late Father William Cunningham, co-founders of Focus: HOPE in Detroit; Steve Mariotti, founder of the National Foundation for Teaching Entrepreneurship in New York; and all the others who perform miracles on a shoestring.

- My superb executive assistants over the last twenty-five years: Sue Bailey at Cummins, Sheryl Smith and Erika Hrabec at the University of Michigan, Louise Alitto at Alger, and Kate Metz and Joyce Williams at the University of Illinois.

I also want to thank:

- Liz Barry of the Life Sciences Institute at the University of Michigan, and my brother-in-law, Dave Decker, both of whom read early drafts of the book and encouraged me to keep going, and Paul Courant, former provost of the University of Michigan and a partner in leadership, who supported this endeavor.

- Dr. Phil Margolis, who has provided me with wise guidance for many years; Nick and Elena Delbanco, who inspired me to write through their writing and support; and Marty and Nancy Zimmerman, wonderful friends in every way.

I want to acknowledge members of my family for making my professional life possible and my personal life a joy: my wife, Mary; our children and their spouses, Brian and Leisa White and Audrey and Darren Imhoff; and my grandchildren, Bernie and Hattie White.

Finally, I thank the members of the board of trustees of the University of Illinois for entrusting me with the leadership of the great university for which they have ultimate responsibility: Chairman Lawrence C. Eppley; trustees Devon C. Bruce, Frances G. Carroll, David V. Dorris, Dr. Kenneth D. Schmidt, Niranjan S. Shah, Marjorie E. Sodemann, Robert Y. Sperling, and Robert F. Vickrey; student trustees in 2005–2006 Shumail Alam, Carrie Bauer, and Nicholas Klitzing; as well as Treasurer Lester H. McKeever, Jr. and Secretary Michele Thompson.

B. Joseph White
Urbana, Illinois
October 1, 2006

ABOUT THE AUTHORS

B. Joseph White is currently president of the University of Illinois. A native of Detroit, reared in Kalamazoo, he earned his bachelor's degree, *magna cum laude*, from the Georgetown University School of Foreign Service in 1969 and an MBA, with distinction, from Harvard University in 1971. He also earned a doctorate in business administration in 1975 from the University of Michigan. White joined the University of Michigan faculty as assistant professor of organizational behavior and industrial relations in 1975; was associate professor from 1978–1980; associate dean in the U-M Business School from 1987 to 1990; interim dean 1990–1991; president of the U-M William Davidson Institute 1993–2001; dean of the Business School 1991–2001; and interim president in 2002.

White also has private-sector experience, including six years at Cummins Engine Co., Inc., 1981–1987, first as vice president for management development and then as vice president for personnel and public affairs. White is an independent director or trustee of several companies, including Equity Residential, headquartered in Chicago; Gordon Food Service; and Kelly Services. He is a director of the W.E. Upjohn Institute for Employment Research. He has chaired the boards of several large healthcare organizations, including the University of Michigan Health System, St. Joseph Hospital in Ann Arbor, and the Catherine McAuley Health System. He is currently a member of the American Council on Education's Board of Directors.

Mr. White has written, taught and lectured extensively on leadership, management, and organizational matters. He and his wife, Mary, are the parents of two grown children and have two grandchildren.

Yaron Prywes is currently an organizational consultant with GHL Global Consulting, LLC, and is pursuing a doctoral degree in social-organizational psychology at Columbia University. Mr. Prywes earned his bachelor's degree from the University of Michigan specializing in Middle Eastern politics, and holds a Master of Arts in Organizational Psychology from Teachers College, Columbia University. His expertise is in strategic organization change with particular interests in leadership, diversity, and team-building. He lives in New York City.